Eco-Theological Significance of Water

Christian Heritage Rediscovered

The Series, as the name suggests, is meant to focus on Christian Faith & Living vis-à-vis topics like Literature & Poetry, Indigenous Philosophizing, Ethical response towards Agriculture, Health & Healing, Science & Technology, Ecofeminist Theology, Sociological approach towards Human Rights, Law & Politics, Arts, History of Ideas, Ancient Civilizations, Cultural Contiguity, Religious Cosmologies & Mysticism, Footsteps of famous Theologians, World Peace & Harmony, Global Capitalism, Network Marketing, Cybertheology, Population & Demographics, Epigraphic Studies, Contextualized Education, and many others. We welcome a Mss. on any topic/s mentioned, whether they are original works, scholarly monographs, collections of conference papers, revised dissertations, or translations of historical documents. Through the Series we, the Publishers, are striving to put forward published works that may help Institutions, Academic Bodies, Researchers, Scholars and the World at large in furthering their respective knowledge and understanding on the concerned subject. We welcome your comments on our efforts and further suggestions on how we can foster the upcoming thoughtful theologically grounded books.

Christian Heritage Rediscovered - 21

Eco-Theological Significance of Water

A Critique on Privatization in the Indian Socio-Economic Milieu

Rev. T. P. Salim Thanka Kumar

CWI

Christian World Imprints™

First Published in 2015 by

Christian World Imprints™
Christian Publishing & Books from India
H-12 Bali Nagar, **New Delhi-110015**
info@christianworldimprints.com
www.ChristianWorldImprints.com
Phone: +91 11 25465925

ISBN-13: 978-93-5148-066-2 (HB) 978-93-5148-078-5 (PB)

Cataloging in Publication Data--DK

Courtesy: D.K. Agencies (P) Ltd. <docinfo@dkagencies.com>

Thanka Kumar, T. P. Salim, 1977- author.
Eco-theological significance of water : a critique on privatization in the Indian socio-economic milieu / T.P. Salim Thanka Kumar.
pages cm. -- (Christian heritage rediscovered ; 21)
Includes bibliographical references (pages) and index.
ISBN 9789351480662 (HB)
ISBN 9789351480785 (PB)

1. Water--Religious aspects. 2. Ecotheology--India. 3. Water--India. 4. Drinking water--Social aspects--India. 5. Drinking water--Economic aspects--India. 6. Privatization--India. 7. Water in the Bible. 8. Theology--India. I. Title. II. Series: Christian heritage rediscovered ; 21.

DDC 201.77 23

Printed at Chawla Offset Printers

Dedication

With all Glory to God
I dedicate this book
to my beloved parents
Mr. A. Thankappan and
Mrs. S. Pushpabai
who nurtured and
inspired me for all success

Christmas, 2014

The Book

The book carefully unpacks the hegemonic discourses that shield the ideology of neo-colonialism deeply entrenched in the intentions of privatization of water resources. The author's sensitive and sustained critique of privatization of water unearths the pitfalls of water management in India. This intellectual work also undertakes a study on the significance of 'water' in various religions, such as Hinduism, Islam, Buddhism, Sikhism, Zoroastrianism, Judaism apart from Christianity. Major issues like water management, water pollution, waterborne diseases, ground water, climate change, water in relation to women and children, water in relation to dalits and tribals, privatization of water, and many more, have been dealt with, in detail.

There have been numerous research works on this subject, but the present one differs as theological critique on privatization of water being its main thirst. The biblical-theological discernment has been employed as a yardstick to make the critique stronger. This research formulates a comprehensive view of the problem enabling a critical response and making the Christian faith community realize the need to be responsible to defend water from the emerging jeopardy.

This book is grounded on a subject that needs immediate attention so as to secure the welfare of the most vulnerable communities in India. It has a prophetic vision which calls the

Church, as a part of society, to respond vigorously in eradicating the evil forces of privatization of water in India. It is meant for Ecologists, Socio-Economists, Christian Laity, Church Clergies, Religious Leaders, Policymakers, Researchers and Students, alike.

The Author

Rev. T. P. Salim Thanka Kumar is a Presbyter in Church of South India in the Diocese of Kanyakumari. He hails from the village Elanchirai of Kanyakumari District. After completing his school education he has obtained his Bachelor degree in Economics from (Nesamony Memorial Christian College, Marthandam) Manonmaniam Sundaranar University, Tirunelveli. After his B.A. he obtained B.D. from the United Theological College, Bangalore in 2004 and gained the degree from the Serampore University. He has completed his M.Th. in Christian Theology at the Tamilnadu Theological Seminary, Arasaradi, Madurai and obtained the degree from the Serampore University in 2009. He has also obtained his M.A. degree in Sociology from Manonmaniam Sundaranar University, Tirunelveli in 2012. He has joined in the pastoral ministry in 1998 and got his presbyter ordination in 2010. He is interested in applied theology and in the public theological discourse.

Foreword

I'm delighted and pleased that my former student, now a public theologian, Salim Thanka Kumar's work on water and its privatization is being published. I am proud to have been asked to provide a Foreword to this work. In a context where one of the most precious and vital resources that should be available freely to all people, the commercialization of water, water production and distribution, coupled with age-long discrimination in terms of so-called purity and pollution not only "muddy the waters" but deprive vast sections of our society of the possibility of healthy living and human dignity, when they are forced to scrounge for this resource and contend with the barricades, both metaphorical and real, that control access to this life-element, this work is both opportune and crucially important.

One of the incredible realities of the Christian faith is that of our belonging to the one body and the fact that we are bound and connected to one another in ways that we scarcely imagined and hardly every think about. Our immediate situation takes center stage – after all, aren't we part of particular groups, bound by ties of class and caste, blood and birth, with our joys and sorrows, opportunities and challenges? Should the struggles and challenges of those outside our affinity groups be of concern to us, when their pains are not our pains, and their experiences are not our experiences? Well – what when their struggles, challenges, sorrows, and experiences are because of decisions that we have made and alliances that we have forged? If we truly affirm that we belong to one body, then we have to recognize that this means that we have to reckon with the reality that we are interconnected beings, and the health of the body depends on the health of those who comprise that very same body. If a vast section are deprived of resources that should be available to all, this is not only a sign of deeply unhealthy relationships, but a poison that will affect all those who are part of the body, even though some of us would prefer not to think about this and even deny that this is so, while wallowing in what we consider plenitude available to us. But, are we prepared to count the cost? Have we recognized that we are part of the larger vision of unity and stewardship, a vision that reaches to the ends of the earth, a vision in which the least, the last, and the lost are welcomed, with us, to the overflowing abundance of the table of our Lord, where there is food and drink, including water, for all?

Do we really believe, do we care to believe, that we are part of a cosmic vision of healing, health, and wholeness that God intends for all God's people? We are called upon to be stewards of the abundance of God's riches, celebrating God's gifts, and sharing God's bounty in the midst of the disorderliness and untidiness of everyday life. It is precisely in the midst of this messiness that we experience the reality of the depth and riches of God's grace, grace that is so abundant, so overwhelming in the way in which it overflows, so invasive in terms of how indiscriminate it is, that we can only respond with gratitude and wonder, gratitude because unworthy though we be, we have been found worthy to be called companions of Jesus, and wonder that in spite of who we really are, God calls us to the ongoing task of being ambassadors of God, ambassadors testifying to God's ongoing love for all humankind, and ambassadors offering our hearts, our hands, our resources, our abilities, our talents, indeed, all that we are, to working in solidarity with the poor and marginalized, and recognizing that in experiencing their hospitality, including cold water on a hot day, we are indeed invited to experience the hospitality of God.

This is remarkable – as remarkable as the reality that we are called into this circle of solidarity, with people that we know and are familiar with, and with people that we don't know, may not care to know, people who are very different from us, people whom we may or may not want to invite into our charmed circles, but people who are loved by God and called into solidarity with all of us, so that freely forgiven and generously welcomed, we can challenge the structures that privatize water, confess our role in creating these barriers, and work to dismantling them as redeemed and consecrated people. Can we recognize our calling to be in solidarity with all God's people for the sake of the world? As we read this work and ponder on the implications, my hope is that we will recommit ourselves to the task of courageously testifying to the harsh realities that so many of our fellow human beings and the wider creation groan under, recognizing that this groaning is part of the groaning of God's spirit, longing for the restoration of the interconnectedness of all God's creation, and with this recognition move forward in faith and action, so that the concerns that this work bears witness to will not be in vain, and that, in reality, a non-commodified understanding of the centrality of water in all our lives will lead to a fresh and renewed appreciation of the meaning of the water of life.

Rev. Dr. J. Jayakiran Sebastian
Dean of the Seminary and
H. George Anderson Professor of Mission and Cultures
The Lutheran Theological Seminary at Philadelphia
Philadelphia, PA, USA

Christmas 2014

Acknowledgements

I thank God, the Almighty, for guiding and molding me all through the years, especially, in doing this work. I am greatly indebted to many people who have helped me in completing this work. I am obliged to Rev. J. Oliver Stanley for being my mentor both in my ministerial formation and studies. I am thankful to my teacher, Rev. Dr. Ivy Singh, of the Tamilnadu Theological Seminary, Madurai for her support during this work.

My special thanks are due to Rev. Dr. J. Jayakiran Sebastian, my former teacher at the United Theological College, Bangalore for encouraging me for this work and writing the 'foreward' for this book. I am thankful to my friend Rev. Dr. Allan Samuel Palanna, Chairperson, Department of Theology and Ethics of the United Theological College, Bangalore for helping me meritoriously in this work. I would like to record my gratitude to Rev. Dr. Charles Singaram, my teacher for promoting my theological thinking as his student. My sincere thanks to my friends, Thomas M. J., Sam Varghese, Chacko Laji and Rev. Rohan Gideon, for their support during this work.

I am grateful to Mr. Sudhanshu Kanda of the Christian World Imprints for the efficiency and attention paid towards publishing this book.

I am indebted to my parents, Mr. A. Thankappan and Mrs. S. Pushpabai, to my sisters - Kumari Helen Rani, Kumari Pushpa Rani and brothers - Anil Thanka Kumar, Bibin Thanka Kumar for their prayers and support in many ways. I am grateful to my parents-in-law, Mr. S. Lawrence and Mrs. J. H. Darling Sarojam, and my brother-in-law, Shine D. Lawrence, for their prayers, love and support that they extended towards my studies.

Finally, I am thankful to my beloved wife, Shini Lawrence, for being selfless in extending her love, prayers and encouragement in every possible way in doing this work and in my life. I appreciate my daughter, Jessie Sashni, for cheering me up with her smiles and love.

May all glory and honour be to the Lord God Almighty always!

Introduction

Life, the way we know it, is not possible without water.[1] Water is now being increasingly referred to as the 'blue gold' in analogy with crude oil, which is termed as 'black gold.'[2] Water is an essential source of life. Without which the earth is nothing but an arid desert, a land of hunger and thirst where human beings and beasts are doomed to death. Water is directed towards the earth for common use by all, including human and other living creatures. Human beings categorize water based on its usage in the order of priority such as: drinking water, livelihood water, industrial water, and leisure water.[3]

1. Statement of the Problem

In India, drinking water is being privatized under the umbrella of neo-liberalization. This, in turn has affected the basic living conditions of the people. Therefore, there is a critical need to respond to this issue

1 Astrid Hardtke, "Privatizing God's Treasure for the World," *Water: God's Gift for Life* (Geneva, Switzerland: World Alliance of Reformed Churches, 2006), 47.

2 Angela Saini, "Scarce 'blue gold'," *Frontline* (February 13, 2004), 37.

3 *Leisure Water* is used in golf courses, swimming pools and other water sports. ["Water Sustains Life," *Statement on Water* (A Statement of the Conference on "Land, Water, Air – People Struggling for Life in a Globalising Economy" held in Bangalore on 10-15 Dec.2001), *National Council of Churches Review* CXXII/1 (January – February 2002), 121].

theologically. Therefore, this study seeks to address the dangers of water crisis and to preserve the sanctity of water through a theological engagement in the significance of "Water of Life".

2. The Crisis Intensified

Water is surely the central condition of life on earth and the basis of survival of all creatures on our planet. However, nature is increasingly subjected to domination and exploitation. Water, the unique substance that gives life to our planet, has become a highly scarce resource. It is becoming inaccessible for common use by all creation. Parts of the world have too much or too little of it. In other places it is polluted or unequally distributed. Rapid population growth, combined with industrialization, urbanization, agricultural intensification, and water-intensive lifestyles are resulting in alarming water crisis.

Moreover, today, government and private companies are misusing water by privatizing and exploiting it under neo-liberal ideology. Misappropriating water by vested interests consequently led to water crisis in many ways. In India, present day water crisis has brought socio-economic, cultural, and devastating ecological imbalances. Commodification of water has resulted in water pollution, depletion of ground water levels, water related diseases etc. Furthering of this attitude of human beings toward water will lead to questionable future of life. Therefore, eliminating the dangers of water crisis and conservation of water resources, need to be affirmed.

The increased awareness of water scarcity and the privatization of dwindling natural resources have given rise to new social movements, initiated by the affected communities across the country today. These new struggles have the dimensions of economical, ecological and social aims to protect livelihoods, defend basic rights and reject the commodification of water and other resources. At the same time, these dimensions safeguard common heritage and natural resources against the onslaught of economic globalism. These struggles, by and large, are guided by a common ideological commitment that natural resources like water belong to the earth and all species for all time and must therefore continue to remain a common property resource. These struggles are also emerging as a major rallying point in defending the communities' right to water and life.[4] These aspects have boosted up the possibilities of making critical response in the research.

Furthermore, the campaign launched by United Nations, "Water for Life 2005-2015" for safe clean water, a secure and close supply and improved sanitation for the world's population[5] throws more light into the context of the research.

3. Scope and Limitation

This research would help to enhance the theological significance of water, and to respond theologically to the perils of water-based life. Accordingly, this research has attempted to critique privatization theologically by examining the claims of the ideology of neo-liberalization. Biblical-theological perception also provided a major role for the scope of the research. The discussion involved in this research, however, is limited to the Christian perspective though it has included, to a certain extent, the significance of water from other faiths. Giving importance to drinking water, this research also considered the seriousness of other uses of water in life.

4. Previous Research

Earlier the United Nations had declared 1981-1990 as the decade of "International Drinking Water Supply and Sanitation." But recently, after United Nations announced 2005-2015 as the decade of "Water for Life" campaign, studies on 'water' has gained momentum. Limited studies on water in consultation levels have been done. World Alliance of Reformed Churches' (WARC) Executive Committee which met on October 2005 in Evian, France had reflections on the theme "Water – God's Gift for Life." In India, the UELCI[6] National Theological

4 Ann Kathrin Schneider and Uwe Hoering, *King Customer? The World Bank's "new" Water Policy and its Implementation in India and Sri Lanka* (Mumbai: Vikas Adhyayan Kendra, 2005), v.

5 Clifton Kirkpatrick, "Introduction to the Theme," *Water: God's Gift for Life*, edited by Judi Fisher (Geneva, Switzerland: World Alliance of Reformed Churches, 2006), 8.

6 United Evangelical Lutheran Church in India.

Colloquium which met on May 3-9, 2004 in Ooty, Tamilnadu had a discussion on the theme "Water as Life: Water as Right," in effect which produced a book entitled *Waters of Life and Death: Ethical and Theological Responses to Contemporary Water Crises* edited by Sam Peedikayil Mathew & Chandran Paul Martin. Some studies on water and its related issues in India have been done. Few works on 'water' to be noted are: V. J. John's *Water Struggle* (Edited), Ramasamy R. Iyer's *Water: Perspectives, Issues, and Concerns*, Vandana Shiva's *Water Wars: Privatization, Pollution and Profit* and Solomon Victus' *An Analysis of the Drinking Water Crisis in Madurai City and the Relevance of People's Struggle: A Theological Reflection* – a thesis written to the Senate of Serampore College (M.Th., 1991, Unpublished). Few articles also have been written on 'Water.'

This research differs from the previous in dealing with the theology of water in the context of privatization of water in India. The theological critique on privatization of water is the main thrust of this research. This research formulates a comprehensive view of the problem enabling a critical response and makes the Christian faith community realize the need to be responsible to defend water from the emerging jeopardy.

5. Methodology of the Research

This research is primarily based on the perspective of eco-theology. The research is done by combining an inter-disciplinary method to make the crucial links between the biblical text and the prevailing context. To a certain extent, the research stays within the sociological nuances by using related sources to analyze the context of privatization of water in India. Biblical-theological discernment became a yardstick to make the critique stronger. In the course of the study, it also engaged in the task of deciphering the multifarious interpretations of key concepts such as 'neo-liberalization' and others involved in the discussion.

6. Definitions

Drinking water: The traditionally given definition is that it is potable water that is vital to maintain the various systems in the body. Drinking is in order to satisfy the thirst. Not for casual or luxurious drinking. This research has taken the wholeness of the term "drinking water" to mean that the whole creation, not only human, needs water for survival, that is, primarily for drinking. Water, on its whole meaning primarily meant for drinking only. Thus, this study has taken this term in this sense by also giving importance to other necessities of water in life. The terms such as 'fresh water' and 'clean water' are also used interchangeably.

Water of Life: Water of life is primarily meant to say water that gives life, that is for drinking, the intake by all creatures, including human beings. By this it does not reduce any qualities of water. In this research all possible means are integrated to say that water constitutes every aspect of life.

Neo-liberalization: Neo-liberalism is a comprehensive term which is explained as "a set of economic policies that have become widespread during the last 25 years or so. Neo-liberalism has been imposed by powerful financial institutions like the International Monetary Fund (IMF) and the World Bank."[7] 'Neo-liberalism is an ideology and a philosophy in which the existence and operation of a market are valued in themselves, separately from any previous relationship with the production of goods and services, where the operation of a market or market-like structure is seen as an ethic in itself.'[8] However, the beliefs and lives of the Indian people are being taken under this shade of neo-liberalism. With its false creeds this ideology misleads people as if it leads towards a new kind of liberalizing economy. The term "neo-liberalism" is considered as an umbrella term for an ideology like, privatization. The process of bringing people into this ideology is referred as neo-liberalisation.

Eco-theology: Eco-theology is generally considered as a part of Christian ethics, which deals with the Christian understanding of Nature and Creation, especially the Christian responsibility in safeguarding the natural environment. It is often an anthropocentric theology where the life of human beings alone is focused on. In this

7 Cited by John Mohan Razu, "Water for People, Water for Life: An Ethical (Christian) Response," *Waters of Life and Death: Ethical and Theological Responses to Contemporary Water Crises*, edited by Sam Peedikayil Mathew & Chandran Paul Martin (Delhi: ISPCK & Chennai: UELCI, 2005), 21-22.

8 *Ibid.*, 25.

eco-theology, the perspective goes further from an anthropocentric eco-theology to a life-centered eco-theology in which the lives of both, human as well as non-human creatures are included.

7. The Structure of the Research

This research is divided into four chapters. The first chapter undertakes a study on the significance of 'water' in various religions, such as, Hinduism, Islam, Buddhism, Sikhism, Zoroastrianism, Judaism, and Christianity. By its due momentousness in life, water plays a central role in many religions and beliefs around the world. In the mentioned religions, water is signified in various aspects such as: water cleans the body, and by extension purifies it, these two main qualities confer a highly symbolic, even sacred, status to water. Water is, therefore, a key element in ceremonies and religious rites and by no means water is degraded in any religion.

With an overview of India's water crisis, the second chapter discusses different water-allied issues in the present Indian society. Today, water stress hits India in a ghastly way. Water-related issues increase every day in new forms. Privatization of water affects the economy of common people and creates modern crisis. Consequently, water crisis became a major threat to survival of not only humans but also other creatures. This chapter carries major issues such as, water management, water pollution, water-borne diseases, ground water, climate change, water in relation to women and children, water in relation to Dalits and Tribals, water and human rights, water policies of India, water conflicts, and privatization of water. From this, we understand that a wise and community-based management and use of water would help us to reduce certain problems and would aid us in exercising our fundamental duty to protect water from the evils of privatization. The point is that in India, the measures to protect drinking water, though they are set in the form of rights and policies, they have to be re-viewed and rephrased from a common citizen's outlook.

Having discussed the issues associated to water, an attempt is made in the third chapter to probe into the possibilities to make theological critique on privatization of water with "water of life" as its basis under the umbrella of ecological perceptions. Drinking water is to satisfy the thirst of all creatures. Therefore, the quest here is to make critique on the evil forces which do not allow the creatures, including humans, to satisfy their thirst. This chapter deals with privatization at a larger level. Further the corollaries of privatization of water, such as, economic, social, ecological, and health- related consequences are underscored. Bottled water is taken as a moral issue within the limits of the critique. Theological critique on privatization of water is done beginning with various theological affirmations on water, such as, patristic theology, process theology, and theology of the sacraments, eco-theology, and eco-feminism.

Considering biblical-theology as a primary tool, critique is made with water as source of all life, and drinking water, by its virtues, is the life sustaining and nurturing force. Ownership over resources is discussed with the principles of common heritage where water is an inherited resource from God and thus God as the owner is emphasized. Further, mainly, privatization of water is critiqued as 'Leviathan,' a gigantic evil power, a symbol of death. Privatization with its leviathanic nature disrupts and creates turmoil in the regular flow of life. Privatization is also criticized as a neo-colonialism. Theological insights like, water represents God's presence is also emphasized. Water of life is taken as the theology of life, which extends towards a theology of water. To contravene and challenge this evil power one has to consider water not as a commodity but life-maker. Therefore, we have to change our view from anthropocentrism to life-centeredness where the life of all creatures is acknowledged. We also need to be reminded that privatizing water is equal to privatizing God, the source and the giver of life through water.

Finally, the fourth chapter takes the discussion further to reflect theologically. Primarily the theological significance of water as a symbol of life imports its reality in Indian context. When water and the poor people of India groan for liberation we ought to move towards an alternate economy, which gives importance to people and sustainability of all resources where God, the Economist provides God's household to the creation for their livelihood. Also, we need to form community ownership of water as we had in before. Finally, a paradigm shift from growth model to *Shalom* model, which creates the well being of all creation including humans where water gets its due respect, is proposed in order to share water with all creation and give life to all. Therefore, with its prophetic vision, Church, being part of the society, called to respond practically to root out the evil forces of privatization of water from India.

Contents

Foreword xi

Acknowledgements xv

Introduction xvii

Chapter 1: Significance of Water in Different Religions 1

Introduction 1

1.1. Water in Hinduism 2

1.1.1. In Purification 3

1.1.2. Water as Divine 3

1.1.3. Water in Vedic Tradition 4

1.2. Water in Islam 6

1.2.1. Types of Purification 7

1.3. Water in Buddhism 9

1.4. Water in Sikhism 10

1.5. Water in Zoroastrianism 10

1.5.1. Water in consortium with *Varuna* 12

1.5.2. The Laws of Purity 12

1.5.3. The Sacred Bath - *Nahn* 13

1.5.4. The *Naojote* Ceremony 13

1.5.5. Marriage Ceremony 14

1.5.6. Water as Divine 14

1.6. Water in Judaism 15

1.6.1. The *Mikveh* *15*

1.6.2. The Great Flood Story 15

1.6.3. The Red Sea Event 16

1.7. Water in Christianity 16

1.7.1. Baptism 16

1.7.2. Holy Water 17

1.7.3. Ablutions 18

1.7.4. Water in the Bible 18

Conclusion 18

Chapter 2: Water-Allied Issues in India 21

Introduction 21

2.1. Water Crisis in India 22

2.2. Water-Allied Issues in India 23

2.2.1. Water Management 23

2.2.2. Water Pollution 25

2.2.3. Water-Borne Diseases 31

2.2.4. Ground Water 32

2.2.5. Water and Climate Change 33

2.2.6. Water Conflicts 34

2.2.7. Water and Women & Children 35

2.2.8. Water and Dalits & Tribals 37

2.2.9. Water and Human Rights 37

2.2.10. Water Policies of India 40

2.2.11. Interlinking of Rivers 42

2.2.12. Dam Constructions 44

2.2.13. Privatization of Water 45

Conclusion 46

Chapter 3 : "Water of Life" as Cornerstone for Theological Critique on Privatization of Drinking Water in India 47

Introduction 47

3.1. Drinking Water 48

3.2. Privatization 48

3.3. Privatization of Water: An Overview 49

3.4. Privatization of Water in India 51

3.4.1. Two levels of Privatization 51

3.4.2. Corollaries of Privatization of Water 52

3.4.3. Bottled Water: A Moral Issue 55

3.4.4. Why Oppose Privatization of Water? 57

3.5. Theological Critique on Privatization of Water 58

3.5.1. Various Theological Affirmations on Water 59

3.5.2. Biblical-Theological Critique 63

3.5.3. Water of Life is Theology of Life: Towards a Theology of Water 74

3.5.4. How to Contravene and Challenge this Evil Power? 75

Conclusion 78

Chapter 4: Theological Reflections of Water and its Significance in the Indian Context 79

Introduction 79

4.1. Need for a Theological Reflection 80

4.2. Water as a Sign and Symbol 80

4.2.1. Hermeneutical Approach of Christian Theology 81

4.2.2. Water as a Symbol of Life 81

4.3. Indian milieu 84

4.4. Groaning for Liberation 85

4.5. What Can be Done? 86
4.5.1. Towards an Alternate Economy 86
4.5.2. Community Ownership of Water 88
4.5.3. A Paradigm Shift from Growth Model to *Shalom* Model 89
4.6. How Best Can We Respond to Water Issue? 90
4.6.1. Church's Response 91
Conclusion 93
Conclusion 95
Bibliography 99
Index 113

Chapter 1

Significance of Water in Different Religions

Introduction

From the perspective of the discipline religions, water is one of the cosmic hierophanies[1], like sky, earth, stones, etc. Their description elucidates the dialectic of the sacred on the one hand, and what sort of forms the sacred will take on the other.[2] Water symbolizes the

---

1 Hierophany is a term designating the manifestation of the sacred. The term is derived from the Greek *hiero*, which means "sacred," and *phainein*, which means "to show." The term refers to any manifestation of the sacred in whatever object throughout history. Whether the sacred appear in a stone, a tree, or an incarnate human being, a hierophany denotes the same act: a reality of an entirely different order than those of this world becomes manifest in an object that is part of the natural or profane sphere [Mircea Eliade and Lawrence E. Sullivan, "HIEROPHANY," *Encyclopedia of Religion*, edited by Mircea Eliade, vol. 6 (New York: Macmillan Publishing Company, 1987), 313].

2 Mircea Eliade, *Patterns in Comparative Religion* (London: Sheed and Ward, 1971), xii-xiii.

primal substances from which all forms come and to which they will return. It is the principle of what is formless and potential, basis of every cosmic manifestation and container of all seeds. It is always germinative, containing the potentiality of all forms in their unbroken unity. It will always exist; it existed at the beginning and returns at the end of every cosmic or historic cycle.[3] In cosmogony, ritual and iconography, water fills the same function in whatever type of cultural pattern we find it, *precedes* all forms and *upholds* all creation.[4]

Water plays a central role in many religions and beliefs around the world. As source of life, it represents (re)birth. Water cleans the body, and by extension purifies it, and these two main qualities confer a highly symbolic, even sacred, status to water. Water is, therefore, a key element in ceremonies and religious rites. To be apparent in the perspective of religions, this chapter undertakes a study on the concept 'water' from various religions in India.

1.1. Water in Hinduism

The sacredness of water receives perhaps the greatest emphasis in Hinduism. According to its teachings, the "waters of life" are believed to bring humankind the life force itself.[5] There is an ancient Hindu dictum, which says, "The earth is our mother, and we are all her children"[6] whereby it affirms that water is blood of the mother earth. Water has a special place in Hinduism because it is believed to have spiritually cleansing powers. Although, Hinduism encompasses so many different belief systems, the one most that Hindus do share is the importance of striving to attain purity and avoiding pollution.[7]

3 *Ibid.*, cited by K. P. Aleaz, "Waters in Vedic-Post Vedic Traditions," *Water Struggle,* edited by V. J. John (Kolkata: Bishop's College & Delhi: ISPCK, 2007), 35.

4 Mircea Eliade, *Patterns in Comparative Religion,* 188.

5 Senator Al Gore, *Earth in the Balance: Ecology and the Human Spirit* (London: Houghton Mifflin Company, 1992), 261.

6 *Ibid.*

7 Jayati Chakravarthi, "Water in Religions," *Humane Response to Water Crisis,* edited by D. John Chelladurai (Nagpur: India Peace Centre, 2006), 59.

Water is one of the five great elements in Hinduism.[8] Also, Hindus use water in all their religious activities and ceremonies as a source of energy as well as a powerful medium for purification.[9] Flowing water is believed to be even more pure and sacred and having a bath in the waters of the rivers, such as, the Ganges, Yamuna, Narmada, Godavari, Kaveri, Sarasvati, and Sindhu, is a sacred act. Thus, water is not only one of the five elements, but essential for meditation and worship.[10]

1.1.1. In Purification

For Hindus, morning cleansing with water is a basic obligation. *Tarpana* is the point at which the worshipper makes a cup with his/her hands and pours the water back into the river by reciting the mantras. After sipping some water, he/she may, then, apply the distinguishing mark of his *sampradaya* (tradition), and say the morning prayer, *samdhya*. *Sodhana* is Hindu purification and is necessary for different reasons and at different levels. Physical purification is a part of daily ritual which may, in the case of *sadhus,*[11] be very elaborate. *Sodhana* is also necessary if caste rules have been broken, for example, if someone drinks from the same vessel as a member of a lower caste, and before *puja*. Every temple has a pond near by and devotees are supposed to have a bath before entering the temple.[12]

1.1.2. Water as Divine

The qualities and powers of water are explained in various ways. Waters are often bound up with divine powers. The Hindu world generally holds them to be goddesses. More explicitly, in other cases, it is the sea, certain rivers, and certain springs that are considered

8 The five great elements are: Space, Air, Fire, Water, and Earth. They are, in Hinduism, called as *pancamahabbhuta*.

9 Hindus sprinkle water over themselves before going into a temple, before sitting for meditation or before offering a prayer.

10 Dwivedi and B. N. Tiwari, *Environmental Crisis and Hindu Religion* (New Delhi: Gitanjali Publishing House, 1987), 32.

11 *Sadhus* are Hindu holy people who renounce the world seeking Brahman.

12 Jayati Chakravarthi, "Water in Religions," 60.

to be gods. People in Vedic India, for instance, sacrificed to rivers.[13] Because of the immanence of divine power within this liquid element, water can be perceived as the divinity itself.[14] While highlighting the importance of water to human's life, Jean Rudhardt says:

> *"Water is essential to human's life; it ensures his/her nourishment by fertilizing the land. It is more than nourishment, since it is the source of nourishment. It may, therefore, be compared not only to milk, but more particularly to the cow. Because of its utility, it is perceived as a privileged support to vital forces."*[15]

The rivers and their confluence became places of pilgrimage in ancient cultures. Ceremonies of initiation and death were and still are performed at these places. It is because of their life-giving and life-fulfilling properties that the appellation "mother" is bestowed on such rivers as Mother Ganga.[16] The *Gautama Dharmasutra* says: "One must not splash water with his feet nor enter water when one is full of dirt; one must not discharge into water blood, excreta, urine, spit, and semen."[17]

1.1.3. Water in Vedic Tradition

Moreover, Vedas portray water's different qualities and forms in different places. In *Rigveda*, water is great and all-pervading. It is treated as the first principle and appears as a "dark undulation" (*Aprak etam Salilam*).[18] *Atharvaveda* considers water as 'propitious' and the

---

13 Jean Rudhardt, "Water," *Encyclopedia of Religion*, edited by Mircea Eliade, vol.15 (New York: Macmillan Publishing Company, 1987), 354-355.

14 *Ibid.*

15 *Ibid.*, 356.

16 Seshagiri Rao, "The Five Great Elements (*Pancamahabhuta*): An Ecological Perspective," *Hinduism and Ecology: The Intersection of Earth, Sky and Water*, edited by Christopher Key Chapple and Mary Evelyn Tucker (NewDelhi: Oxford University Press, 2000), 33.

17 *Ibid.*

18 In *Rgveda* 10.82.1 it appears as the primeval slime in which heaven and earth were plunged in the beginning, and in 10.72.4-6 it is mentioned as the "wave-surge": *Apah* (water), which were certainly great, pervaded all, holding the embryo, and producing *Agnih.* Water is also mentioned as an invigorating

"enhancer of power."[19] *Yajurveda* (2.20.7) elucidates the importance of *Yajnas* to purify the waters as follows: "Human offerings in *Yajnas* purify the water sucked by the sun in clouds with the air. Then that water rains and makes the medicine on earth sound."[20]

1.1.3.1. *APAH*, the Sacred Waters

In Hindu myths, the waters are divided into three: the primordial waters (*Agre apah*), the divine waters (*Apo devih*), and the waters of life (*Ujre dadhatana*). Water, as a primordial symbol, is treated as sacred in the Hindu myths. "The waters are *pratistha*, the underlying principle."[21] That is, from the waters the whole universe is produced. These waters are portrayed as "*Hiranyagarbha*, the womb of the seed of all creation,"[22] and as "the womb of *Brahmanda*, the cosmic egg from where Brahma, the creator arose."[23] The divinity of waters is seen in the sleeplessness of its flow from the depths and through the channels dug out by men, having Ocean as their goal; its clearness as crystal; from whom all deities drink exhilarating strength.[24] As a

---

source of pleasure and tranquility, as the possessor of life's infusing power, and as having medicative healing power, which contains all medicines (See O. P. Dwivedi and B. N. Tiwari, *Environmental Crisis and Hindu Religion,* 30).

19 *Atharvaveda* 3.13.5 says: "The water are propitious, the water verily are the enhancer of power. These water, truly, do support Agni and Soma. May the readily flowering, strong sap of the honey-drops (waters) come to me, together with life's breath and luster" (See O. P. Dwivedi and B. N. Tiwari, *Environmental Crisis and Hindu Religion,* 30).

20 O. P. Dwivedi and B.N. Tiwari, *Environmental Crisis and Hindu Religion,* 31.

21 *Satapatha Brahmana* 14.3.2.13. See Frans Baartmans, *APAH, The Sacred Waters: An Analysis of a Primordial Symbol in Hindu Myths* (Delhi: B. R. Publishing Corporation, 1990), 214.

22 Frans Baartmans, *Ibid.*

23 "Long ago, when all things animate and inanimate were lost in one dreadful ocean there appeared a large egg, source of the seed of all creatures. Lying in this egg, Brahma went to sleep. At the end of a thousand Ages he awoke" (*VaSa*, 22.17-22). See Frans Baartmans, *Ibid.*

24 Raimundo Panikkar, *The Vedic Experience Mantramanjari: An Anthology of the Vedas for Modern Man and Contemporary Celebration* (London: Darton, Longman & Todd, 1977), 118-119.

life-giving symbol, water is the source of all life and particularly, it is there for us to drink.[25]

By summing up the long Vedic tradition, the Indian texts, such as, *Bhavisyottarapurana* and *Satapatha Brahmana* say that, water is the source of all things and of all existence; waters are the foundations of the whole world; they are the essence of the plant life, the elixir of immortality like *amrta*; they ensure long life and creative energy, they are the principle of all healing, and so on.[26]

Thus, the attitude of Hinduism towards water is highly respectable. Hinduism relates the origin of rivers with their God. It is believed that the river Ganga springs from the foot of Lord *Vishnu*, the preserver God and the temples of ancient India have been dedicated to the rivers that are believed to originate from Lord *Shiva*'s hair. Hinduism believe that by dipping themselves in the rivers they will be discharged from all of the sins.[27] Apart from these beliefs there are some popular traditions prevailing among the Hindu peasants of Tamilnadu to glorify the rain God and water which are the central part of their life.[28] In Hinduism, therefore, water has a significant role as it is portrayed in various places and as it is believed so.

1.2. Water in Islam

In Islam water is important for cleansing and purifying. It is declared by Quran that "we have created everything from water."[29] It is also important for Muslims to have the ritual purification before the performance of the *Salat*, the prayer, which is one of the five basic

25 Raimundo Panikkar, *The Vedic Experience Mantramanjari: An Anthology of the Vedas for Modern Man and Contemporary Celebration* (London: Darton, Longman & Todd, 1977), 119.

26 Mircea Eliade, *Patterns in Comparative Religion,* 188.

27 Solomon Victus, "A Theological Reflection on Water," *Waters of Life and Death: Ethical and Theological Responses to Contemporary Water Crises*, edited by Sam Peedikayil Mathew & Chandran Paul Martin (Delhi: ISPCK & Chennai: UELCI, 2005), 258-259.

28 One of those is that, till today, in Tanjore on the 18th day of the Tamil month *Adi*, the river Cauvery water will be released and in the mean time in the presence of the District High Officials, the peasants sprinkle variety of grains on the new water (See *Ibid.*, 259).

29 Senator Al Gore, *Earth in the Balance,* 261.

devotional practices.[30] In *salat*, the ablutions are important and obligatory and ritual purification is the key of prayer. The need for such purification is mentioned both in Quran and Hadith. The Quran establishes the principle: "O ye who believe! Draw not near to prayer… till ye have bathed"(4:43). The traditions greatly elaborate the idea with such phrases as "Religion is built on cleanness" and "Purification is one-half of faith." The physical acts are to symbolize the cleansing of the heart.[31]

1.2.1. Types of Purification

There are three forms of purification: (1) *Wudu*, the lesser ablution; (2) *ghusl*, the greater ablution and (3) *tayammum*, a special purification by sand in the absence of water.[32] But generally differentiate with the first two.

1.2.1.1. *Wudu*

This is the lesser and most common ablution. Outside most mosques and near to the entrance, one can see a washing area, a shallow pool of water, where the worshipper may perform the required ablution. If the worshippers are at home or at work, they may use whatever facilities are available for cleansing. The stages of the ablution are as follows: Washing the hands to the wrist thrice, reciting one's intention; rinsing the mouth thrice; washing the nostrils thrice; washing the face; washing the hands to the elbows thrice, the water running to

30 The five basic devotional practices of Islam are called as 'the five pillars of Islam,' or 'the pillars of obedience.' These are: 1) *Tashahhud*, the confession of faith, 2) *Salat* or *namaz*, reciting the daily prayers, 3) *Saum* or *roza*, observing fast, 4) *Zakat*, the almsgiving, 5) *Hajj*, undertaking the pilgrimage to Mecca [cf. Bevan Jones, *The People of the Mosque*, 5th edition (Delhi: ISPCK and Madras: CLS, 1980), 96]. Among these, the *salat* is the formal fivefold daily prayer, accomplished by physical actions, which is the liturgical prayer of Islam. Though there is another prayer called *dua*, which is a voluntary form of petition to God, generally the word *salat* is used for prayer in Islam [see. Roland E. Millar, *Muslim Friends: Their Faith and Feeling – An Introduction to Islam* (Chennai, India: Orient Longman, 2000), 212].

31 *Ibid.*, 217.

32 Bevan Jones, *The People of the Mosque*, 5th edition (Delhi: ISPCK and Madras: CLS, 1980), 97.

the elbow; passing damp hands over the whole head; rubbing wet fingers in the ears, behind the ears, and through the beard; rubbing wet fingers of one hand between the fingers of the other; washing the feet, wet fingers between the toes. When the washing is complete, the believer may carry the Holy Quran, do the prayers, and participate in other spiritual activities.[33]

1.2.1.2. *Ghusl*

This is the greater ablution, which requires a full bath in pure water, after declaring the intention to do so. Muslims are obliged to perform *ghusl* after sex which incurs a state of major ritual impurity. *Ghusl* is also recommended before the Friday prayer, the two main feasts, and before touching the Koran.[34] Here, water must be poured three times over the right shoulder, three times over the left, and finally three times on the head. Besides this, there is threefold regulation: the mouth must be rinsed; water must be put in the nostrils, and the whole body must be washed. Not one hair must be left dry in the process.[35]

1.2.1.3. *Tayammum*

This is a special purification by sand or earth, which is prescribed for special circumstances.[36]

Thus, Muslims consider water as the gift of God, which cannot be privately owned or monopolized according to Islamic law.[37] In Islam, therefore, water has a great reverence and it is given a more

---

33 Roland E. Millar, *Muslim Friends: Their Faith and Feeling – An Introduction to Islam* (Chennai, India: Orient Longman, 2000), 217-218.

34 Jayati Chakravarthi, "Water in Religions," 61.

35 Bevan Jones, *The People of the Mosque*, 98.

36 These special circumstances include when water is not procurable within two miles; when one is sick and the use of water might be dangerous; when water cannot be obtained without encountering danger from an enemy, wild beast or reptile; when a person, delayed by some festival or funeral, has no time for the ordinary ablutions (see. *Ibid.*, 98-99).

37 Ziauddin Sardar, Islamic Futures: The Shape of Ideas to Come (London: Mansell Pub., 1985), 230, cited by Solomon Victus, "A Theological Reflection on Water," 260.

or less sacred place in the religious rituals. When the availability of water is not there, then only they can go for an alternative, which is proposed by the religion. Thus, clear water is a vital symbol in Islam.

1.3. Water in Buddhism

The basic attitude of Buddhism towards natural resources seem to be the same as that of Islam. The glaring difference between Islam and Buddhism is that Islam emphasizes external purity, whereas Buddhism emphasizes internal purity.[38] In Sri Lanka, the monks sprinkle sanctified water on the person who suffers from evil spirit and over the areas, which are affected with epidemic diseases, along with chanting certain selected sacred texts.[39] Rites are basically absent. Water does, however, feature in Buddhist funerals where water is poured into a bowl placed before the monks and the dead body. As it fills and pours over the edge, the monks recite, "As the rains fill the rivers and overflow into the ocean, so likewise may what is given here reach the departed."[40]

From the scriptural insights of Buddhism (*Dighanikaya*, Vol.III, 80-89), it can be understood that, in the evolutionary process of the world, water played a major role. That is, "there was a time when the whole planet was covered with water."[41] In the course of time, "land emerged from water."[42] Water, thus, played an important role in the creation of the cosmos. Also, since the nature and its elements are interconnected with the life of human beings, Buddhism advocates respect to nature. Moreover, Buddha's life-philosophy demands every believer's close communion with nature.

38 Nalinaksha Dutt, *Early Monastic Buddhism*, second edition (Calcutta, 1971), 252, cited by Solomon Victus, *Ibid.*, 260-261.

39 Lynn de Silva, *Buddhism: Beliefs and Practices in Sri Lanka*, second revised edition (Colombo, 1980), 111, cited by Solomon Victus, *Ibid.*, 261.

40 Jayati Chakravarthi, "Water in Religions," 57.

41 Lily de Silva, "Man and Nature in a Mutual Causal Relationship," *Man in Nature: Guest or Engineer?*, edited by S.J. Samartha and Lynn de Silva (Colombo: The Ecumenical Institute for Study and Dialogue & Geneva: The World Council of Churches, 1979), 7.

42 *Ibid.*

1.4. Water in Sikhism

In Sikhism, ecological and environmental concerns are expressed vividly through the writings of Guru Nanak. In the Sikh world view, God is the creator of all and is revealed through His creation, which includes water. While expressing the reverence for nature and for God's creation, Nanak significantly designated water as the progenitor. At another time, he stated that the nature or creation is important to one's life. Human life is significantly aided with air, water, and earth. Therefore, if water sires us, then dumping our garbage into our rivers would be unforgivable.[43] Also the Sikh scripture, *Granth Sahib*, says that human beings are composed of five elements of nature in which "water teaches us purity."[44] According to Sikhism, human beings need an awareness of the sacred relationship between human and total environment, such as earth, air, water.

1.5. Water in Zoroastrianism

Zoroastrians believe that water is pure and sacred, and so pollution is evil. Zoroastrians themselves must avoid pollution of any kind and must perform ritual ablutions before saying their prayers[45] and before any religious ceremonies such as weddings.

Purity and pollution are central concerns in Zoroastrian thought and practice. For minor pollutions, *padyab-kusti* is performed, which involves washing and saying special prayers. On special occasions such as weddings or initiations, *nahn* is performed which combines *padyab-kusti* with the symbolic eating of a pomegranate[46] leaf and the drinking of *nirang* (ritual cow's urine) for spiritual cleansing. This is followed by the prayer of repentance, the *Patet*, and finally a bath. Serious pollution, for example, contact with a corpse, requires the nine day *baresnum* ceremony which is held in the temple precincts

---

43 I. J. Singh, *Sikhs and Sikhism: A View with a Bias* (New Delhi: Manohar Publishers, 1994), 146-147.

44 Senator Al Gore, *Earth in the Balance,* 261.

45 Prayers are said five times a day facing a source of light.

46 The pomegranate had a symbolic association in antiquity with fertility and eternal life [See Cyrus R. Pangborn, *Zoroastrianism: A Beleaguered Faith* (New Delhi: Vikas Publishing House, 1982), See f.n.23 in p.93].

and includes periods of prayer and washing with the aid of priests.[47] Zoroastrian ethics clearly insists that the sacred element, water should not be polluted through contact with impure things such as a dead body.[48] Water is to be looked with care and reverence, because it is an instrument of purification.[49] The punishment amounts to four hundred stripes, where a man who has touched a corpse touches water without being cleansed. If a person willfully carries dead matter to water, he is worthy of death.[50] The sanctity of water is very important to Zoroastrians. People must not urinate, spit or wash one's hands in a river or allow anyone else to. Along with fire and earth, water must be kept pure.

These creations are the means by which worshippers can approach Ahura Mazda[51] and by which Ahura Mazda can approach his worshippers. *Haurvatat*[52] is the creator of water. *Haurvatat* is represented by consecrated water used in priestly acts of worship. The holy day of *Haurvatat* and water is in midsummer and people pray and make offerings by the seashore or any natural water. In everyday life, *Haurvatat* is observed by keeping water unpolluted and being temperate and self-disciplined.[53]

---

47 Jayati Chakravarthi, "Water in Religions," 63-64.

48 *Vendidad*, VI. 26, 41, cited by Maganlal A. Buch, *Zoroastrian Ethics* (Baroda: A. G.Widegery, 1919), 102.

49 *Arda Viraf*, 155; 162,163, cited by *Ibid.*, 103. In Zoroastrian ethics, both water and fire are considered as sacred elements, and therefore, both should not be polluted but looked to with reverence. Here, for the significance of the research I use only the element, water.

50 *Vendidad* VIII.104, 106 and *Sad Dar*, 336, cited by *Ibid.*, 174-175.

51 Ahura Mazda is the main God. The Zoroastrians believe in six benevolent divine beings known as Amesha Spentas, which with God's Holy Spirit, Spenta Mainyu are linked with God's (Ahura Mazda's) creation, certain priestly rituals, observances by laypeople and the seven holy days of obligation. The Amesha Spentas are believed to dwell within each of their creations while at the same time remaining aspects of God's nature. Each *Amesha Spenta* protects its creation and represents an aspect of Ahura Mazda and a feature of the good creation (See Jayati Chakravarthi, "Water in Religions," 64).

52 *Haurvatat* means wholeness, health and integrity. It is a feminine being. It is the personification of what salvation means to the individual (*Ibid.*).

53 Jayati Chakravarthi, "Water in Religions," 64.

1.5.1. Water in consortium with *Varuna*

When we read the pagan background of Zoroastrianism, particularly, of gods, it is clear that water has been associated, predominantly, with *Varuna*. This connection is very close and is said that "the primary concept of *Varuna* was that of a personification of the waters themselves."[54] Moreover, "water indeed, peculiarly belongs to *Varuna* in all its manifestations. Therefore, he is addressed as 'Child of the Waters,' and water is reverenced as holding him, and hence water is used to invoke his presence."[55] *Varuna* also has an attribute as 'God of the Waters.'[56]

1.5.2. The Laws of Purity

In Zoroastrianism, the laws of purity maintains water as one of the venerated elements, as fire. It is also an object of the Zoroastrian cult. Since it is the creation of *Haurvatat*, it must be kept pure, and therefore, to use it to wash away dirt is an impiety. Hence no impure objects, such as, excrement, blood-soaked clothes, a dead body, are allowed to come into contact with a natural source of water such as lake, stream or well; and nothing ritually unclean is washed there. Instead water is drawn off to limit the pollution.[57] Moreover, while insisting on the stewardship of human beings to the world, the purity laws say that human beings are supposed to keep themselves meticulously clean…but when they are unclean they should not plunge recklessly into the clean element of water, forgetting their duty as stewards of this world.[58]

---

54 Mary Boyce, *A History of Zoroastrianism*, Vol. I (Netherlands: E. J. Brill and Leiden, 1975), 33.

55 *Ibid.*

56 For this, the interpretation is given through the name *Varuna*. The meaning of the root word *ver* (means, 'bind,' or 'tie') of the name *Varuna* is given as 'binding utterance,' or 'oath.' This oath is the solemn truthful affirmation which constrains a man. The interpretation is that through the oath *Varuna* got this secondary trait (See. *Ibid.*, 33-35).

57 *Ibid.*, 296.

58 *Ibid.*, 297.

1.5.3. The Sacred Bath - *Nahn*

As the concerns of purity are explicitly defined through the rules of rituals of the religion, to uphold purity the ritual bath is required. The ritual and the sacred bath or a kind of purification in the religious ceremonies or rites in Zoroastrianism is known as *Nahan* (or *Nahn*).[59] This bath is highly important, which is followed in different ceremonies, like, initiation (*Naojote*) and wedding. In the act of this bath, the first bathing agent is the gomez, which is the urine of an ordinary bovine, then fine sand, and finally, the consecrated water. Each of these agents is rubbed over the body three times. Finally, a more complete bath is taken with water.[60]

1.5.4. The *Naojote* Ceremony

The initiation of a Parsee (Zoroastrian) child into the fold of the Zoroastrian religion is known as *Naojote*[61] (*Navjote* or *Naojate*). The ceremony of the initiation consists of the investiture of the child with a sacred shirt called *sudrah* and a sacred thread called *kusti*. After this initiation only a Zoroastrian child is said to be responsible for the duty of offering prayers and observing religious customs and rites as a Zoroastrian. The age of a child for this ceremony is seven.[62]

A little before the time of the proper ceremony, the child is made to go through the sacred bath, *Nahan*. The sacred ceremonial bath with consecrated water in the *Naojote* has the signification among the Parsees (Zoroastrians), as that, which the bath with the sacred water of the spring of Calirhoe (or Enneacrunos) had among the ancient Athenians, or that which the bath with the sacred water of Ismenus had among the Thebans.[63]

---

59 Jivanji Jamshedji Modi, *The Naojote Ceremony of the Parsees*, 2nd edition (Bombay: Fort Printing Press, 1914), 3.

60 Cyrus R. Pangborn, *Zoroastrianism: A Beleaguered Faith* (New Delhi: Vikas Publishing House, 1982), 93.

61 *Naojote* is a term deriving from an older one indicating a "new birth."

62 Jivanji Jamshedji Modi, *The Naojote Ceremony of the Parsees*, 1, 2.

63 *Ibid.*, 3.

1.5.5. Marriage Ceremony

The sacred bath is an imperative in the marriage ceremony. On the wedding day itself, the couple prepare for the evening ceremony by taking the sacred bath, *Nahn*.[64] Only when the *Nahn* is over, either the groom or the bride is allowed to wear the new clothes and traditional outfits. Thus, this bath is a prerequisite for wedding ceremonies.

1.5.6. Water as Divine

For Zoroastrians, water is the great purifier. More than that water is deified in Zoroastrianism. John Wilson, while discussing about the Parsi religion, says, "the water named *Areduisur* (literally, the lofty), as it is known among the Parsis,[65] is the giver of purity. It is the strength of young-men; it is the *foetus* in women; it is the milk of women. Therefore, there is no doubt that this doctrine has originated in the deification of water."[66] Thus, water is given a divine status in the religion.

Apart from this, in the writings of Herodotus about the laws and manners of the Persians there are references that they sacrificed to water.[67] Other accounts also say that they worship water and sacrifice particularly to water and fire[68]. In the great liturgy of the Parsis, it is said that "I invoke, I celebrate ... the *waters*...,"[69] and one of the

64 Cyrus R. Pangborn, *Zoroastrianism,* 90.

65 Zoroastrianism was for a long time the official religion of Persia, from 521 BC on the accession of Darius I. Eventually, however, the Muslims destroyed the Persian kingdom in AD 642, and they somewhat forcibly converted the majority to Islam, and persecuted those who were loyal to their religious faith. Many of the latter decided to emigrate to Western India in order to pursue their beliefs and forms of worship without opposition. Thye settled mainly in the area of Bombay (Mumbai). Today, there are only a very small remnant (possibly some 10,000) of Zoroastrians left in Iran, and they are usually refered to as Gabars, or infidels. Those who settled in India are called Parsis (Parsees), that is, 'the people of Pars' (i.e. Persia) [See. Ivor Morrish, *The Thoughtful Guide to Religion* (New Delhi: Pentagon Press, 2007), 95].

66 John Wilson, *The Parsi Religion* (Gurgaon, Haryana: Vintage Books, 1989), 311.

67 *Ibid.*, 182.

68 *Ibid.*, 191.

69 *Ibid.*, 259.

prayers say that "I worship all the *fountains of water*, flowing and stationary."[70] Thus, in their polytheistic belief, the Zoroastrians (the Parsis) worship and adore the natural elements, including water.

The significance of water in Zoroastrianism is a combination of its purifying properties and its importance as a fundamental life element. Therefore, while water is used in purification rites and rituals it is sacred itself and so it must be kept from being polluted. It must be preserved in its sacred purity.

1.6. Water in Judaism

1.6.1. The *Mikveh*

In Judaism, ritual washing is intended to restore or maintain a state of ritual purity, called *mikveh*. *Mikveh* means 'gathering' of water and the ritual bath. Its origin can be found in the scriptural text: "Only a spring, cistern, or collection of water shall be clean" (Leviticus 11). 'shall be clean' is understood by the Rabbis to mean 'shall be cleansing,' that is, one who has suffered contamination remains unclean until he/she has immersed himself/herself in the *mikveh*.[71] These ablutions can be: washing the hands, the hands and the feet, or total immersion which must done in 'living water', i.e., the sea, a river, a spring or in a *mikveh*. In Temple times, ablutions were practiced by priests, converts to Judaism as part of the initiation rites and by women on the seventh day after their menstrual period. Priests had to wash their hands and feet before taking part in Temple services. The ritual washing of hands is performed before and after meals and on many other occasions.[72]

1.6.2. The Great Flood Story

The story of the Great Flood is told in Genesis 6-8. God destroyed humanity by sending a great flood. Only Noah and his family and a pair of each animal were saved in the ark built by Noah. Afterwards,

---

70 John Wilson, *The Parsi Religion* (Gurgaon, Haryana: Vintage Books, 1989), 262.

71 Louis Jacob, *The Jewish Religion: A Companion* (Oxford, New York: Oxford University Press, 1995), 347.

72 Jayati Chakravarthi, "Water in Religions," 61-62.

God promised he would never attempt to destroy the earth again and sent the rainbow as a sign of this covenant. The story of a Great Flood is also found in other cultures such as the Australian Aborigines and some Pacific Islanders. The Israelites' story is different to these because it emphasizes the ethical demands of God. The flood is a divine punishment from which Noah survives because of his moral worthiness. The Flood washed away all the sins of the world so that we could start afresh. This is echoed in Christianity by the death and resurrection of Christ that eradicates sin so that nothing will stand in the way of human and God.[73]

1.6.3. The Red Sea Event

The Red Sea is significant in Jewish history because its parting by Moses was a miraculous event at the beginning of the Exodus which enabled the Israelites to escape from the Egyptian army that was chasing them. God allowed Moses to part the sea so that the Israelites could walk safely to the other side on dry land, while the Egyptians drowned as the sea came together again. This miracle was a reward for the faith of Moses and the Israelites, God's Chosen People. The parting and crossing of the Red Sea shows that God has power over nature, even the mighty oceans. Water here is powerful, but an instrument of God for punishment (for the Egyptians) and blessing (for the Israelites).[74]

1.7. Water in Christianity

1.7.1. Baptism

Almost all Christian churches or sects have an initiation ritual involving the use of water. Baptism has its origins in the symbolism of the Israelites being led by Moses out of slavery in Egypt through the Red Sea and from the baptism of Jesus by John, the Baptist in the Jordan. After Jesus' resurrection he commanded his disciples to baptize in the name of the Father, Son, and Holy Spirit (Matthew 28:19-20). Baptism is regarded differently in different denominations within Christendom. Baptism is a symbol of liberation from the

73 Jayati Chakravarthi, "Water in Religions,"62.

74 *Ibid.*, 63.

oppression of sin that separates us from God.[75] However, Christians are baptized in water, as a sign of purification.[76]

The use of water is important for its own symbolic value in three ways: it cleanses and washes away dirt, fills everything it enters as God fills those who are immersed in Him and we need water to survive physically as we need God to survive spiritually. In the early church, baptism was usually performed with the person standing in water and with water being poured over the upper part of the body. This was called 'immersion' but today the term refers to the method of dipping the whole body under water which is used, for example, by the Baptist and Orthodox churches. In most Western churches today, the rite is performed by pouring water over the head three times and sometimes sprinkling water over the head.[77]

Another important significance of water for Christianity is the "living water" that Jesus described himself as. John 4:1-42 is the story of Jesus and a Samaritan woman to whom he offers living water so that she will never thirst again, in other words eternal life through him.

1.7.2. Holy Water

Holy water is water which is blessed for use in certain rites, especially that which is blessed at the Easter Vigil for baptism of catechumens. The use of water other than for baptism goes back to the 4th century Eastern and the 5th century Western churches. The custom of sprinkling people with water at mass began in the 9th century. At this time 'stoups', basins for holy water from which people could sprinkle themselves on entering a church, were in common use.[78]

---

75 Jayati Chakravarthi, "Water in Religions," 57.

76 Senator Al Gore, *Earth in the Balance*, 261.

77 Paula Abrams, *Water in Religions*, http://www.africanwater.org/religion.htm accessed on 25/07/2008.

78 Jayati Chakravarthi, "Water in Religions," 57-58.

1.7.3. Ablutions

Ablutions in Christianity are mainly baptism and the washing of fingers and communion vessels after the communion (in some traditions). This takes place in two parts. Firstly, the chalice is rinsed with the wine, and then the chalice and priests' fingers with wine and water. This ablution is important because after the bread and wine has been consecrated, Christ is believed to be present.[79]

1.7.4. Water in the Bible

Water has become the main component as well as symbol in the faith interpretations of the people of the Biblical era. In the Bible, water was also important for cleansing. Priests were washed at their consecration (Exodus 29:4); special ablutions were demanded for priests on the Day of Atonement (Leviticus 16:4, 24, 26) and of all men for the removal of the ceremonial pollution (Leviticus 11:40; 15:15; Deuteronomy 23:11). Also, water is associated with many aspects. It is associated with danger and death (Psalm 32:6); with warfare (2Kings 3:19-25); God's favour; and as symbolic of God's blessings and spiritual refreshment.

Conclusion

From its presence before creation of the world, water has a highly respectable position in the major religions of India. Among the above stated religions, water has a major role to play in the act of purification. Though it is used in the rituals as a medium of purification, it signifies the purity and cleanliness of hearts of the believers. Water is regarded as sacred for it gives a real meaning to the one who uses it. It should be understood that "any use of water with a sacred intention brings together reintegration and creation."[80] Also, when water is used in a ritual it becomes holy after it is blessed, as in the Baptism of Christianity.

Moreover, water is given a divine status in some religions and it is equated with deities like, *Varuna*. More than that water is being worshipped and sacrifices are being offered to water. Water is also

79 Paula Abrams, *Water in Religions*.

80 Frans Baartmans, *APAH, The Sacred Waters,* 210.

portrayed as a life-giving force. It is the source of all life. Since, it is used for drinking it becomes more significant in the life of all creation. As "at every level of existence water is a (the) source of life and growth"[81] it is needed everywhere.

On the whole, from its attributes and qualities it gives the idea that water is a hierophany. Therefore, human beings are not given a power either to misuse it or to have power over it. Rather it should be understood that since water is a life-centered factor there is a need to create a pertinent atmosphere for the sustainability of all living creatures.

81 Frans Baartmans, *APAH, The Sacred Waters,* 211.

Chapter 2

Water-Allied Issues in India

Introduction

Water, the unique substance that gives life to our planet, has become highly scarce resource. Parts of the world have too much or too little of it. In other places, it is polluted or unequally distributed. Rapid population growth, combined with industrialization, urbanization, agricultural intensification, and water-intensive lifestyles are resulting in a global water crisis.

According to S.M. John Kennedy, "About 20 percent of the population currently lacks access to safe drinking water while 50 percent lacks access to a safe sanitation system. Falling water tables are widespread and cause serious concern, both because they lead to water shortages and, in coastal areas, to salt intrusion. Both, contamination of drinking water and nitrate and heavy metal pollution of rivers, lakes, and reservoir are common problems throughout the world. The world supply of fresh water cannot be increased. More and more people are becoming dependent on limited supplies of fresh water that are more polluted. Water scarcity, like food security, is becoming a major national and regional priority in many areas of the world. Conflicts are worsening; pollution is unabated; ground water levels continue to fall; rivers are drying up; and there is no sign of greater efficiency or prudence in using water."[1] Thus, water crisis is becoming a major threat to survival of not only humans but also other creatures.

2.1. Water Crisis in India

Water is the biggest crisis that India is facing in terms of spread and harshness. This crisis affects one in three people in cities and villages. Already it has been reported that in Chennai, Bangalore, and Delhi, water is rationed. With the lives and livelihoods of millions at risk, the nightmare has worsened. India's population is expected to touch 1,650 million by 2050, which means the demand for water will rise from 634 bem now to 1,447 bem. Nearly, two-thirds of this will be for irrigation, as India would need to double its food production from the current 200 million metric tonnes to 450 million.[2]

The demand for fresh water is increasing sharply and rapidly because of the growth of population, the pace of urbanization and the process of economic development. The pressure on the available supply is likely to become more severe.[3] Moreover, industry and commerce tend to pollute and contaminate rivers, aquifers and public supply systems.[4] Not only that, ground water is virulently affected by the bore wells through which industries suck up water from underground. These are visible in the cases of Tamil Nadu, Kerala and Chhattisgarh.[5]

1 A. Vaidyanathan, "Imperatives of Water Governance," *The Hindu*, March 20, 2004, 10, cited by S. M. John Kennedy, "Pure Water is the Fundamental Right of All," *Journal of Dharma* 31/4 (October-December 2006), 487.

2 *Ibid.*, 489.

3 Ramaswamy R. Iyer, *Towards Water Wisdom: Limits, Justice, Harmony* (New Delhi: Sage Publications, 2007), 18.

4 *Ibid.*, 134.

5 In Tamil Nadu, places like Tirupur and Palar basin water is used for economic uses, such as in textile and leather industries. They take away water from, and make water unusable for, basic needs and sustenance livelihoods. In Kerala, in Plachimada, the bore wells of the Coca-Cola Company are said to have an impact on the water sources of the surrounding villages. In Chhattisgarh, the leasing of a stretch of River Sheonath to a corporate body seems to undermine

However, the crisis of water is basically due to the improper treatment of water and related resources. Factors like, hysterical pollution, improper management, extracting more ground water and misusing water for profit motive lead to water stress in a country like India. However, though the Indian government is striving forward to avail equal access to water for all, through various modes, it is being done by exploiting the resource. At this juncture, it demands us to deal with the geopolitical issues. With this overview of India's water crisis, let us look into the different water-related issues in the present Indian society.

2.2. Water-Allied Issues in India

In the midst of the water crisis in the country, the issues pertaining to that have to be given attention. Some of the important issues related to water in India are discussed in the following pages.

2.2.1. Water Management

In India, we need to keep the highest possible standards in the management of the country's water resources. If the water management is poor then the result could be in all areas of life. B.B. Vohra, in his book *Managing India's Water Resources*, notifies that "unless water is utilized to the best possible advantage for enhancing the country's productive capacity, our non-renewable resources of land will not only remain underutilized, and in certain circumstances even unutilized, but will also continue to suffer degradation and depletion."[6] This urges that the precautionary measures have to be taken well in advance in order to shun off from such problems.

To identify and deal with various challenges in the field of water management, Vohra proposes some tasks to which we must address ourselves. They are:[7]

- Complacency must be given up;

---

the community's and even State's control over its natural resources (*Ibid.*, 134-135).

6 B. B. Vohra, *Managing India's Water Resources* (New Delhi: Indian National Trust for Art & Cultural Heritage, 1990), 1.

7 See *Ibid.*, 2-26.

- The country's water resources must be viewed in their entirety if they are to be managed properly;
- Run-off losses must be minimized by aiming at zero soil loss;
- The vast existing unutilized and under-utilized potential of the major and medium sector must be put to optimal use before any fresh potential is permitted to be created;
- Notice must be taken of the complete collapse of the Minor Surface irrigation sector;[8]
- Good agricultural lands must not be permitted to be damaged by water-logging and salinisation;
- The major and medium sector must not be subsidized any longer;
- The present policy regarding floods must be reviewed;
- A more rational and reliable data base must be created for better water management;
- Ground water must be recognized as the most important source of irrigation;
- Water must be used with the utmost efficiency and economy.

For the management of the water resources, even the water policy of India (2002) proposes a participatory approach and the sad part is that it invites the participation of private sector. While giving a critique on the National Water Policy 2002, Sunita Narain[9] said, "The National Water Policy will remain inert and ineffectual because it is far removed from the two simple but important challenges of water management today – rainwater harvesting and community management in this initiative."[10] Leading environmental NGOs and activists hold that India has been hit by water shortages because of a

---

8 Minor Surface Irrigation is defined as projects with commands of less than 2000 hectares each.

9 Sunita Narain is the director of the Centre for Science and Environment (CSE), which has vigorously campaigned for community control over water resources.

10 Ranjit Devraj, "Bypassing community rights: The National Water Policy," http://infochangeindia.org/ 200201015973/Water-Resources/Books-Reports/ Bypassing-community-rights-The-National-Water-Policy.html accessed on 25/07/ 2008.

shift away from traditional methods of storing and using rainwater to exploiting rivers, damming them up through costly and centralized irrigation and drinking water schemes.[11] Thus, reforms are indeed very necessary in the area of water management.

2.2.2. Water Pollution

Water is basic to life. The quality of water determines the quality of life. But owing to massive industrialization, water gets polluted in every form. The toxins from the effluents from major industries seep into and contaminate the ground water to such an extent that water in most of the wells situated in a radius of about 20 kilometers around those factories are not drinkable. Fumes of sulphur dioxide and oxides of nitrogen get incorporated into clouds so much that when it rains, they come down as acid rain.[12]

Water is relatively more prone to pollution than air because it is more viscous, having lesser moment of inertia and possessing loser molecular distance than air.[13] Water is said to be polluted when it is changed in its quality or composition directly or indirectly as a result of waste disposal and other human activities so that it becomes less suitable or harmful for drinking, domestic, agricultural recreational, fisheries or other purposes.[14] The public health service of the U.S. Department of Health, Education and Welfare defines water pollution as: "*the adding to water of any substance, or the changing of water's physical and chemical characteristics in any way which interferes with its use for legitimate purposes.*"[15]

---

11 Ranjit Devraj, "Bypassing community rights: The National Water Policy," http://infochangeindia.org/ 200201015973/Water-Resources/Books-Reports/ Bypassing-community-rights-The-National-Water-Policy.html accessed on 25/07/ 2008.

12 A. Pushparajan, "Environmental Rights: Caring for God's Earth," *Indian Theological Studies* 43/1, (March 2006), 73.

13 P. R. Trivedi and Gurdeep Raj, *Environmental Ecology* (New Delhi: Akash Deep Publishing House, 1992), 482, cited by Laisamma Joseph, "Doordarshan and Its Ecological Awareness Education" (An Unpublished thesis submitted to Madurai Kamaraj University for M.Sc. in Communication, 1998), 28.

14 K. C. Agarwal, *Environmental Biology* (Bikaner, India: Agro Botanical Publishers, 1993), 341.

15 *Ibid.*

Modern civilization is dependent on water for irrigation, industry, domestic needs, shipping and of increasing importance for sanitation and disposal of waste. Most of our water bodies, such as ponds, lakes, streams and rivers have become polluted as a consequence of increasing industrialization, urbanization and other development activities. In India, all the fourteen major rivers including Ganga, Gomti, Cauvery, Damodar and Mini-Mahi are polluted.[16] To expound this reality, Pushparajan in his article, *Environmental Rights: Caring for God's Earth,* cites the example of river Ganga. He says:

> *"Ganga is the largest river basin in India. It is a run of over 2,500 km. three big states (Utter Pradesh, Bihar and West Bengal) are the recipients of major benefits. Its basin has a total population of nearly 45 million. It is no wonder that the fate of such a river has been equated with the destiny of the millions who live on her banks. But it has been estimated that 900 million liters of sewage is dumped into it every day. It is mainly from 27 class-one cities whose waste water is let off into this river. The river that has been considered for centuries the holiest of rivers in India has now turned into one of the filthiest. It is in these circumstances that the Ganga Action Plan was set up in 1985. Under this plan 261 projects were taken up with the only purpose of purifying the river. After a hectic work of 10 years period, the assessment committee reported that the Ganga River was fit for bathing and other purposes except drinking."*[17]

Polluted waters, however, cannot be used for any of the above mentioned uses of human activities, as it is harmful.

2.2.2.1. Sources of Water Pollution

The sources of water pollution are as follows: (i) Sewage and other oxygen demanding wastes, which contain decomposing organic matter and pathogenic agents; (ii) Industrial waste, which contains

16 K. C. Agarwal, *Environmental Biology* (Bikaner, India: Agro Botanical Publishers, 1993), 339.

17 A. Pushparajan, "Environmental Rights: Caring for God's Earth," 73-74.

toxic agents ranging from metal salts to complex synthetic organic chemicals; (iii) Agricultural waste, which comprises fertilizers, pesticides and biocides; and (iv) Physical pollutants, like heat (thermal pollution) and radioactive substances.[18]

2.2.2.1.1. Sewage and other Oxygen Demanding Wastes

Sewage is defined as the waterborne waste derived from home (domestic waste) and animal or food processing plants, and which includes human excreta, soaps, detergents, paper and cloth. This group constitutes one of the largest pollutants of our water. Water pollution is caused by uncontrolled dumping of wastes of villages, towns and cities into ponds, lakes, streams or rivers. If the contamination level is higher, the self-purifying activity of the water body gets lost and water becomes unfit for human consumption and other domestic uses.[19]

A major ingredient of most detergents is phosphate, which combines and inactivates ions such as calcium so that they cannot react with and disable the dirt dissolving molecules. When they discharged into water, the phosphate supports luxuriant growth or blooms of algae. Extensive growth of algae often withdraws great quantities of oxygen from water to the detriment of other organisms, and produces bad odour when decay.[20] The discharge of sewage results into the following:

a) ***Depletion of oxygen contents:*** this is caused by aerobic bacteria in the decomposition of organic matter. The quantity of oxygen utilized by bacteria in degradation of organic substances is called *biological oxygen demand* (BOD). On an average basis, the demand for oxygen is proportional to the amount of organic waste present in water. This BOD value can be used as an indicator of degree of pollution. Moreover, when dissolved oxygen is reduced to low level of water, fish are scarce. Further

---

18 K. C. Agarwal, *Environmental Biology*, 341-342.

19 *Ibid.*, 342.

20 *Ibid.*

deduction of the amount of oxygen results in an increase of anaerobic bacteria.[21]

b) ***Stimulation of algal growth:*** Most of the bloom forming blue-green algae does not seem to be utilized by invertebrates. Biological decomposition of such algal masses in turn leads to further oxygen depletion. In a poorly oxygenated condition, with increased carbon dioxide, fish and other animals die and clean river turns into a stinking drain.[22]

c) ***Spreading infectious diseases:*** Microorganisms, usually viruses, bacteria, some protozoa and helminthes occur in water bodies as a result of sewage disposal therein spread several infectious diseases.[23]

2.2.2.1.2. Industrial Waste

Most of the rivers and fresh water streams which pass near the major cities are polluted by industrial wastes or effluents. These contain a wide variety of both inorganic and organic pollutants such as oils, greases, plastics, plasticizers, methylic wastes, suspended solids, phenols, toxins and other chemical substances, many of which are not readily susceptible to degradation and cause very serious pollution problems. Acid waste and sulphuric acid from coal mines is another serious pollutant that increases hardness of water. It has disastrous effects on life.[24]

In Andra Pradesh, for instance, water pollution through the industries is one of the major problems. It is caused mainly by the Vishaka Steel Plant, thermal plant, the industrial estate and the coal mine. A study conducted by a group of social activists reports that, "in most cases they (people who lived in these areas) are moved away from the traditional sources of drinking water but not provided an alternative. More than two thirds of those affected by mines,

---

21 K. C. Agarwal, *Environmental Biology*, 342-343.

22 *Ibid.*, 343.

23 The common water-borne diseases are Viral hepatitis, Poliomyelitis, Cholera, Typhoid, Paratyphoid, Dysentry, Diarrhoea, Amoebiosis, Giardiasis, Round worm, Hook worm, and Thread worm (*Ibid.*, 345).

24 *Ibid.*, 346.

industries and the thermal plant complained both of water shortage and pollution. Ironically, those who complained of drinking water shortage included about 50% of the persons displaced of major dams that did not replace their traditional sources."[25]

2.2.2.1.3. Pesticides and Biocides

Pesticides are biologically active chemicals used for killing plants or animal pests. Extensive and indiscriminative use of biocides made them an integral part of the biological, geological and chemical cycles of the earth. Today, they are present throughout the ecosystem. Being long-lasting under natural conditions they cannot easily be degraded by microorganisms and physical forces in the environment.[26]

For example, after the use of DDT its residues will stay in the soil and in water. The DDT spread in water may be very low but the aquatic plants will carry more amount of it. As the component of food chain, plants and animals may accumulate DDT in greater concentration in their body. Their body fat will be highly concentrated with this chemical. Then it will get into the blood stream and may cause toxic effect. It will spread from water to fish eating beings, including human beings. This is hazardous to human beings. In human beings DDT is feared to cause cancer.[27]

2.2.2.1.4. Physical Pollutants

Chemical industries, fossil fuel and nuclear power plants use lot of water for cooling purposes and return this water to stream at a higher temperature. The hot water interfaces with the natural conditions in the lake and river effecting aquatic life. This is thermal pollution as heat acts as a pollutant. The thermal pollution is thus the raising

25 Walter Fernandes, et.al., *Development-Included Displacement, Deprival and Rehabilitation in Andra Pradesh 1951-1995: A Quantitative and Qualitative Study of Its Extent and Nature* (New Delhi: Indian Social Institute and Guwahati: North Eastern Social Research Centre, 2001), 156-158, cited by Walter Fernandes, "Land, Water, Air as Community Livelihood: Impact of Globalisation," *National Council of Churches Review* CXXII/1 (January-February 2002), 24.

26 K. C. Agarwal, *Environmental Biology*, 349.

27 *Ibid.*, 349-353.

of temperature of part of the environment (water in this case) by the discharge of substances whose temperature is higher than the ambient. Some plants and animals are killed outright by the water, if it is very hot.[28]

2.2.2.1.5. Eutrophication

Eutrophication is a kind of pollution of fresh water ponds, streams, lakes and so on. In agriculture, the fertilizers are excessively used to promote growth and high yield. These fertilizers contain ammonia, phosphates, nitrites, nitrates, etc., which are washed into the nearby aquatic habits during raining season. The sewage and the industrial wastes also contain such nutrients which accumulate in the nearby lakes or rivers. High concentration of such nutrients stimulates the excessive growth of micro organisms and such other aquatic plants. The micro organisms such as green algae are abundantly found in water, which is known plankton bloom. This increased productivity of fresh water habitats is termed as eutrophication. Eutrophication is hazardous to animals, especially to fish population.[29] Human activity is generally responsible for rapid eutrophication as domestic waste, agricultural and land drainage, and organic industrial waste or their decomposition products reach the water bodies.[30] Eutrophication is, thus, also a serious problem.

However, the situation today is being deteriorated day by day. Ramaswamy R. Iyer rightly observes it that "water pollution is getting out of hand. There are pollution control laws and institutions, but these have not been able to prevent the growing pollution and contamination of water sources and systems, which in effect makes much of the 'available' water resources unusable."[31] He adds, "Water pollution is in fact as great a threat to security as the 'scarcity' about which alarm bells have been ringing."[32] Therefore, water needs to

---

28 K. C. Agarwal, *Environmental Biology*, 355.

29 N. T. Krishnan and G. Santhakumar, *Environmental Biology* (Madurai: J. J. Publications, 1992), 226-227, cited by Laisamma Joseph, "Doordarshan and Its Ecological Awareness Education," 29.

30 K. C. Agarwal, *Environmental Biology*, 356.

31 Ramaswamy R. Iyer, *Towards Water Wisdom...*, 27.

32 *Ibid.*

be protected and its security ought to be affirmed in every realm of life.

2.2.3. Water-Borne Diseases

Water-borne diseases and water-caused health problems are mostly due to inadequate and incompetent management of water resources. Water-borne infection is the common problem of India and the other developing countries. Agarwal reports that, "eighty per cent of the diseases in these countries are linked with contaminated water. Microorganisms, usually viruses, bacteria, some protozoans and helminths occur in water bodies as a result of sewage disposal therein spread several infectious diseases."[33]

Water-borne diseases take millions of lives every year. "It has been estimated that out of the 37 diseases responsible for most deaths in developing countries, 21 are related to water and sanitation. About 1.5 million children under the age of five are estimated to be dying in India each year due to such diseases."[34] These diseases are due to people using contaminated water sources. Lakes and rivers that are used for drinking and bathing in, are often also defecated in and so the diseases spread. Many parasites also live in the water, leading to massive infections. Waterborne diseases include Cholera, Hepatitis A, Tuberculosis, Guinea Worm and many other diarrheal diseases.[35]

A) ***Cholera*:** This is a disease spread by unsanitary conditions and lack of clean drinking water. Its symptoms include diarrhoea, leg cramps and severe vomiting. Around 200,000 cases are reported to the World Health Organization (WHO) each year.

B) ***Hepatitis A*:** This is a liver disease that causes millions of deaths each year, due to ingestion of contaminated water or food.

---

33 K. C. Agarwal, *Environmental Biology*, 345.

34 C. Ramachandraiah, "Drinking Water as a Fundamental Right," *Economic and Political Weekly* (February 24, 2001), 620.

35 http://www.worldvision.com.au/stir/Content.aspx?topicID=478 accessed on 26/08/08. Diarrheal diseases include Giardiasis (Protozoan), Cryptosporidiosis (Bacteria), Campylobacteriosis (Bacteria), Shigellosis (Bacteria), Viral Gastroenteritis (Virus) and Cyclosporiasis (Parasite).

C) ***Tuberculosis*:** TB causes nearly two million deaths annually and the WHO estimates that nearly one billion people will be infected by 2020 if we do not provide better prevention procedures. It is a disease of the lungs and involves chest pain and a bad cough, along with other symptoms.[36]

In addition, water-borne disease can be caused by the pollution of water with chemicals[37] that have an adverse effect on health.

2.2.3.1. Water Scarcity Diseases

Diseases like Trachoma are compounded due to a simple lack of water. **Trachoma** is a highly contagious disease that causes blindness. It is so easily prevented, with just 1 litre of water a day being enough to keep a child's face clean and stop the high rate of infection. Sadly many of the world's poorest people cannot even spare this small amount.[38]

2.2.4. Ground Water

Ground water is the primary source of drinking water. A great majority of rural dwellers' land irrigated with ground water tends to be far more productive than the land irrigated with dam-canal water. But the control of water by TNCs and its involvement in the heavy consumption of underground water led to groundwater depletion from 15 feet to 40 feet.[39] They use high power compressors to suck water from the inner crust of the earth. Thus, over extraction of water resources from underground for commodification causes depletion of ground and destruction of groundwater source. In addition, it

---

36 http://www.worldvision.com.au/stir/Content.aspx?topicID=478 accessed on 26/08/08. Diarrheal diseases include Giardiasis (Protozoan), Cryptosporidiosis (Bacteria), Campylobacteriosis (Bacteria), Shigellosis (Bacteria), Viral Gastroenteritis (Virus) and Cyclosporiasis (Parasite).

37 These chemicals include Arsenic, Flouride, Nitrates from fertilizers, Carcinogenic pesticides (DDT), Lead (from pipes) and Heavy Metals.

38 http://www.worldvision.com.au/stir/Content.aspx?topicID=478 accessed on 26/08/08.

39 John Mohan Razu, "Water for People, Water for Life: An Ethical (Christian) Response," 33.

may cause saltwater intrusion and will damage the source of drinking water. When water is extracted by private companies, it leads to drought on the one side, and it affects not only human beings but also animals, plants and other creatures on the other side. In turn it directs to ecological imbalance.

Furthermore, it is predominantly observed that ground water is being polluted due to industrial discharges at many places. It is also contaminated due to the application of agro chemicals and pesticides for agricultural purposes. It is also noted in various cities that rapid urbanization makes a great impacts on the ground water resources. Samuel Thambusamy notes that, "water is often scarce in urban areas of developing countries. Rapid urbanization increases per capita use of fresh water. Fast population growth with accelerated urbanization, combined with scarce water supplies and poor sanitation, means that governments cannot supply enough water to meet demand."[40] Urbanization demands more water supplies and when the land water sources lacks water there will be more indiscriminate extraction of ground water. Thus, ground water is another existing concern to be dealt with.

2.2.5. Water and Climate Change

The entry of the newer climate change factor compounds the prediction of water shortages in future. Many scientists now believe that water supplies will drastically decrease as deserts expand and evaporation rates increase; rivers will dry up as droughts intensify and the melting of the polar ice caps may lead to the intrusion of salt water into fresh water supplies.[41] The impact of climate change, thus, can be seen on the water resources and economy as follows: less snow fall, slow deposits and glacierization (process of forming glaciers); less rainfall in arid areas, prolonged droughts coupled with excessive precipitation; reduced river flows; reduction in storage of

---

40 Samuel Thambusamy, "Rapid Urbanization in India and Its Impact on Drinking Water Resources: Towards an Action Plan for Engaging Children and Young People in Water Conservation in Chennai," An unpublished article presented in *National Theological Colloquium: Water as Life & Water as Rights, May 3-9, 2004*, 3.

41 Arun Kumar Singh, *Privatization of Rivers in India* (Mumbai: Vikas Adhyan Kendra, 2004), 5.

water in dams; decreased agricultural productivity in arid and semi-arid areas.[42]

The impact of climate crisis on all forms of life is mediated through water in the form of floods, cyclones, heat waves, and droughts.[43] It is the poorest people in the Third World who will be severely affected by climate change, drought, melting glaciers, and rising sea levels.[44] Whether water is life-threatening or life-sustaining depends to a large extent on the ability of climate justice movements to end atmospheric pollution.[45]

2.2.6. Water Conflicts

All over the world, communities in water-stressed countries are beginning to compete with one another for prior use of this precious resource. Tensions are growing across nation-state borders and between cities and rural communities, ethnic groups and tribes, industrialized and non-industrialized nations, people and nature, corporations and citizens, and different socio-economic classes.[46]

It was in the post independence (1947), when India embarked on the construction of large storage reservoirs by replacing "small is beautiful" philosophy of water harvesting with "big is beautiful," started major water sharing conflicts. Since India is an agrarian economy, more than two thirds of population, which has agriculture as its occupation, needs water. When the large-scale storage on the upstream reduces the flow on the downstream there arises the feeling of deprivation of their natural rights. Thus, water conflicts started and when the large diversion increased the conflicts became more pronounced.[47]

---

42 Arun Kumar Singh, *Privatization of Rivers in India* (Mumbai: Vikas Adhyan Kendra, 2004), 7.

43 Vandana Shiva, *Water Wars: Privatization, Pollution, and Profit* (New Delhi: India Research Press, 2002), 40.

44 *Ibid.*, 49.

45 *Ibid.*, 50.

46 Maude Barlow and Tony Clarke, *Blue Gold: The Fight to Stop the Corporate Theft of the World's Water* (New Delhi: Left Word Books, 2003), 64.

47 Vandana Shiva and Kunwar Jalees, *Sujalam: Living Waters. The Impact of the River linking Project* (New Delhi: NAVDANYA, 2003), 63.

The international conflicts are: (a) India-Pakistan conflict on Indus river, (b) India-Nepal conflict on Indus river, and (c) Indo-Bangladesh conflicts. The inter-state conflicts are: (i) conflict between Haryana and Punjab on Ravi-Beas waters, (ii) conflicts between Uttar Pradesh, Delhi and Haryana on Yamuna river, (iii) conflicts between Uttar Pradesh and Bihar over Sone river, (iv) conflicts between West Bengal and Jharkhand on Damodar, (v) conflicts between Karnataka, Maharashtra and Andhra Pradesh on Krishna river, (vi) conflicts between Karnataka and Andhra Pradesh over Telugu Ganga Project (TGP), (vii) dispute between Punjab and Haryana over Sutlej-Yamuna link, and (viii) conflicts between Karnataka and Tamil Nadu over Cauvery river.[48]

The one-day Policy Dialogue meeting on 'Water Conflicts in India' organized by World Water Institute in Hyderabad on the 22nd of March 2005 stated that "Water conflicts arise due to scarcity of water resulting from faulty water management practices. Water conflict is a manifestation of the lack of norms to build consensus for sustained use of water as a common property resource. Water is often used as a measure of control thus power relations in a society make it difficult to resolve conflicts. Competition to access groundwater has resulted in dividing society at all levels. The challenge is to make water a uniting factor and create a water-sharing environment."[49]

2.2.7. Water and Women & Children

In many societies, water is at the core of women's traditional responsibilities such as, in collecting and storing water, caring for children, cooking, cleaning, and maintaining sanitation. These tasks often represent a whole day of work. Sometimes, women have to spend five hours a day for collecting fuel wood and water, and up to four hours for preparing food. Providing access to clean water close to each home can drastically reduce women's workload, and free up time for other more productive economic activities. Water stress leaves women the most vulnerable. Without a ready source of water they may have to walk for several hours every day to find it, or

48 See *Ibid.*, 63-69.

49 http://www.worldwaterinstitute.org/docs/executive%20summary%2022%20march%20meeting.pdf accessed on 25.07.2008.

send their children to fetch it. Child nurturing and education suffer as the available water may be unfit for human use.[50] Thus, women are the most affected ones. Children could also be included in this as they are also forced to go to fetch water and consequently it affects their education.

However, women are not considered in the so-called developmental process, even the policies are silent about them. Walter Fernandes, in his analysis of National Water Policy, says that, "A policy for water management formulated in India in 1987 spoke of it primarily as a resource for irrigation and power. Its first draft did not even mention women who are responsible in most Indian traditions, to ensure the regular supply of drinking water to the family."[51]

Asha Krishna Kumar, in her article 'Women and Water' says that "in every household, particularly in the rural areas, women and the girl children bear the responsibility of collecting, transporting, storing, providing, and managing water. To fulfill this and the added role as the guardians of household sanitation, hygiene and health care, women face considerable stress."[52] She further quotes Sara Ahmad, who expresses that "yet the National Water Policy does not recognize women's role. This is a total denial of women's right to water."[53] Women's life is intrinsically related with water. And they have the traditional knowledge about the sources of water, the ways to use it, to maintain its quality, dependability and limits in storing the resource. They, yet, are ignored from the mainstream of planning and implementing the policies and water programmes.

---

50 S. M. John Kennedy, "Pure Water is the Fundamental Right of All," *Journal of Dharma* 31/4 (October-December 2006), 489.

51 Walter Fernandes, "The Draft Forest Policy 1987; The National Water Policy 1987," *Social Action* 38/1 (Jan-March), 84-94, cited by Walter Fernandes, "Land, Water, Air as Community Livelihood: Impact of Globalisation," *National Council of Churches Review* CXXII/1 (January-February 2002), 18.

52 Asha Krishna Kumar, "Women and Water," *Frontline* 20/20 (October 10, 2003), 77.

53 *Ibid.*

2.2.8. Water and Dalits & Tribals

The separation of Dalits from water resources has been a problem in India. We have to note here that Dalits are considered as lower caste people, impure and untouchables. With these oppressive elements, the upper caste groups deny water to Dalits. They are not even allowed to go near to the water resources for they can pollute the water sources of the upper castes. Dalit women are the main victims of these absurd ideas. Moreover, Tribals, in India, have community ownership of water resources yet the access to water is denied to them. Tribals who live near by water resources are deprived of these resources due to the modern developments, like, dam constructions and their own waters and land are being taken away by the industries. Tribal women, in India, are denied of water much more than that of the other women for they are more responsible in getting water to the domestic purpose. Thus, for both Dalits and Tribals, water, the source of life is denied.

2.2.9. Water and Human Rights

The undeniable fact is that water is basic to humanity. The right to water, therefore, ought to be an immutable aspect of human life. Water being basic to human existence, it is not a right that can be waived, less so can it be appropriated. The presumed legitimacy of statute law has pervasively influenced the nature of the right to water.[54] Usha Ramanathan makes it more clear that, "this treatment of water as an irrigation resource also meant that the right to water got intertwined with the right to land."[55]

In any case, in common law, water is common property. The control over water, therefore, is managed by communities. Community control over common resources represents the only real mechanism for ensuring sovereign control over natural resources. This framework does not determine how community norms function. It merely recognized the rights of communities and hence

---

54 Usha Ramanathan, *Legislating for Water: The Indian Context* (IELRC Working Paper 1992-1) (Geneva: International Environmental Law Research Centre, 1992), 10.

55 *Ibid.*, 11.

opens the legal option of limiting the rights of corporations. National legislation needs to recognize community rights.[56] As Arun Kumar Singh rightly noted, the 'Right' should not be interpreted in terms of the references, but should be treated and considered as a social and cultural good, and also not principals for an economic good.[57]

It is an accepted notion that all human beings, irrespective of their economic background, have a right to use water. Human dignity, life and health, non-discriminative need to be considered as the elements of human rights and applicable for every individual. With regard to the rights of water these elements hold importance. Noted environmentalist Vandana Shiva calls this denial of poor people access to water by privatizing water distribution as terrorism.[58] She further asserts, "Water is traditionally been treated as a natural right. That is, a right arising out of nature, historic conditions, basic needs, or notions of justice. Water rights are natural rights that do not originate with the state; they evolve out of a given ecological context of human existence. By natural rights, water can be used but not owned. People have a right to life and the resources such as water sustain that life."[59] The necessity of water to life is because it brought under customary laws and it has been accepted as natural right is because of the social fact that: "The right over water has existed in all ancient laws, and also the fact that they still continue to exist as customary laws in the modern period, clearly eliminates water rights as being purely legal rights, that is, rights granted by the state or law."[60]

According to the UN, an appropriate meaning to the 'Human Right to Water' entitles everyone to 'sufficient', 'safe', 'acceptable', 'physically accessible' and 'affordable' for individual person and for domestic uses. Also this is to be understood holistically. This

---

56 Usha Ramanathan, *Legislating for Water: The Indian Context* (IELRC Working Paper 1992-1) (Geneva: International Environmental Law Research Centre, 1992), 56.

57 Arun Kumar Singh, *Privatization of Rivers in India*, 121 ff.

58 Vandana Shiva, *Water Wars: Privatisation, Pollution, and Profit*, xiv.

59 *Ibid.*, 20-21.

60 Chattarpati Singh, "Water and Law" (undated memo), cited by Vandana Shiva, *Ibid.*, 21.

includes all rights like, 'Right to Health' not only concentrates the physical aspect of the human community but it includes the 'safe' and 'unpolluted' water too. Water is a limited natural resource and a societal good fundamental for life and health. The 'Right to Water' contains both freedom and privilege.[61] By freedom here it is meant to have 'right to maintain' the access to existing water supply and right to be free from the intrusions to have a basic access to the existing water resources.

2.2.9.1. Safe Drinking Water: A Fundamental Right

Drinking water is a fundamental right that cannot be denied. Initiatives to safeguard and defend drinking water have been taken by different people's movements and people are coming forward to protect the water resources. But, incidents have been noted when people protest to protect their drinking water sources, they were met with brute force.[62]

The Supreme Court of India, however, by quoting Article 21 of the Constitution of India, said that the state is duty bound to provide clean drinking water. The Court ruled that clean drinking water is a fundamental right of all citizens. It said that Article 21 of the Constitution of India guarantees 'Right to Life' and it also includes the 'Right to Clean Drinking Water.' The Court also quoted 1977 resolution of the United Nations Water Conference that pledges access to clean drinking water for everybody, to which India is signatory.[63] Therefore, Water, being part of the global commons, like air, the rights to water should extend to all human beings.

---

61 Christopher Rajkumar, "Right to Water and the Inter Linking of Rivers (ILR): A Critique" (unpublished paper), 3.

62 To mention a few, as Chandramaiah reports, "Police killed three farmers in Falla village in Jamnagar district of Gujrat in December 1999 when they protested against water being taken from Kankavati dam to meet the needs of Jamnagar town ignoring local rural demands. Two farmers were killed in Prakasam district of Andhra Pradesh in February 2000 when they protested against commercial salt farming by an NRI. Groundwater in 14 villages would have been contaminated by saline intrusion due to this farming. Still the NRI got permission (C. Ramachandraiah, "Drinking Water as a Fundamental Right," 621).

63 Arun Kumar Singh, *Privatization of Rivers in India*, 69.

2.2.10. Water Policies of India

For the first time, National Water Policy was adopted in the year 1987, which started with signifying water as thus: "Water is a prime natural resource, a basic human need and a precious national asset. Planning and development of water resources need to be governed by national perspectives."[64] Furthermore, it had water allocation priorities, in which drinking water was given the first priority. It said, "Adequate drinking water facilities should be provided to the entire population both in urban and in rural areas by 1991. Irrigation and multipurpose projects should invariably include a drinking water component, wherever there is no alternative source of drinking water. Drinking water needs of human beings and animals should be the first charge on any available water."[65] Solomon Victus makes a critique that, "it did not use a single sentence about privatization but there were some paragraphs about water pricing and water rates but that too was rationalized with due regard to the interests of small and marginal formers."[66] Moreover, it is evident that such a policy did not propose anything to change the ground realities.

After that the revised National Water Policy was formulated in the year 2002, drawing several criticisms from many quarters. It underscored that water has to be treated as an essential environment for sustaining all life forms; water is a scarce and precious national resource; and the quality of water has to be improved.[67] It also made

64 National Water Policy 1987, clause no: 1.

65 National Water Policy 1987, clause no: 9.

66 Solomon Victus, "Water – A Privatized Commodity…," 9.

67 The National Water Policy 2002 explicitly highlights thus: Water is part of a larger ecological system. Realising the importance and scarcity attached to the fresh water, it has to be treated as an essential environment for sustaining all life forms (clause no: 1.3); Water is a scarce and precious national resource to be planned, developed, conserved and managed as such, and on an integrated and environmentally sound basis, keeping in view the socio-economic aspects and needs of the States. It is one of the most crucial elements in developmental planning. As the country has entered the 21st century, efforts to develop, conserve, utilize and manage this important resource in a sustainable manner, have to be guided by the national perspective (clause no: 1.4); Another important aspect is water quality. Improvements in existing strategies, innovation of new techniques resting on a strong science and technology base

a point of concern with regard to sharing of water resources.[68] Like the 1987 policy, this also had drinking water as its priority. But as Victus looks at 'it does not speak about privatization openly but it encourages private sector participation in water management.'[69] Thus, these policies which have to serve the common people are trying to uphold the external forces that are intruding into the life of the citizens.

2.2.10.1. Influence of the World Bank

India's National Water Policy adopted in 2002 echoes World Bank's thinking and language by introducing a commercial approach to water resources management and drinking water supply.[70] The support of the World Bank to the Indian government in its water projects, though seems like reforming the economy, emphasizes private sector involvement and thus treats water as an economic good. The Bank also gives financial support to the dam projects. The reason for supporting India's dam projects is, it says, "the energy required to secure India's economic growth."[71] This attitude of

---

are needed to eliminate the pollution of surface and ground water resources, to improve water quality. Science and technology and training have to play important roles in water resources development and management in general (clause no: 1.9).

68 Water should be made available to water short areas by transfer from other areas including transfers from one river basin to another, based on a national perspective, after taking into account the requirements of the areas/basins (clause no: 3.5).

69 Solomon Victus, "Water – A Privatized Commodity…," 9. The policy says like this: "Private sector participation should be encouraged in planning, development and management of water resources projects for diverse uses, wherever feasible. Private sector participation may help in introducing innovative ideas, generating financial resources and introducing corporate management and improving service efficiency and accountability to users. Depending upon the specific situations, various combinations of private sector participation, in building, owning, operating, leasing and transferring of water resources facilities, may be considered" (clause no: 13).

70 Ann Kathrin Schneider and Uwe Hoering, *King Customer? The World Bank's "New" Water Policy and its Implementation in India and Sri Lanka* (Mumbai: Vikas Adhyayan Kendra, 2005), vii.

71 *Ibid.*, 37.

financing large-scale dams has had strong criticisms among the non-governmental development organizations both in India and abroad. In a press release, several NGOs complain not only about insufficient transparency and participation of civil society or parliaments in developing the Country Strategy, but also about the Bank's pressure on the Indian Government to approve comprehensive privatization in such important areas such as electricity, water, agriculture and other basic services.[72]

Consequently, when the water policies of India that are influenced by World Bank's such policies it indirectly supports private involvement and does not try to seek any solutions to the water problems in the basic levels.

2.2.11. Interlinking of Rivers[73]

The issue of interlinking of rivers gained momentum on August 14, 2002, when the Indian President in his speech to the nation on the eve of Independence Day, said, "It is paradoxical to see floods in one

---

72 Civil Society Organizations Reject World Bank Country Assistance Strategy, *Press Release*, (August 9, 2004), www.esgindia.org, cited by Ann Kathrin Schneider and Uwe Hoering, *Ibid.*, 38.

73 The historical reading of this project tells us that, it is not at all a new project. In 1881, Arthur Cotton proposed an idea of 'linking of inter-basin water to the linking of rivers and canals to then the British rulers. It was under consideration for a while and then it was rejected The British regime continued for another 66 years in India, but they had never reviewed this Cotton's Proposal. In 1975, Dr. K. L. Rao suggested a similar proposal. The idea was similar to Cotton but it was about the inter-basin transfer of water through *Ganga-Cauvery* and *Bramaputhra- Ganga* link canals. Capt. Dinshaw Dastur forwarded a proposal to make a canal link between the *Himalayan* and Peninsular components with two pipelines in 1980. [Md. Khalequezzaman, "Historic Perspectives of the Indian River-linking Project," retrieved from URL: http://www.e-mela.com/Bangladesh/River_Indian_History_Khalequzza, (2003)]. These two proposals were also rejected under technical and financial grounds. The National Water Development Agency was established in 1982, to explore the feasibilities of inter-basin transfer of water. There was an objection in regard to link the *Bramaputhra-Ganga* basin to the river basins in the rest of the country. Then in 2002 the New Water Policy was proposed and adopted to the country divide in to several water-zones keeping in mind both the surplus and deficit regions. On the eve of Independence Day 2002, the President of India urged for the ILR to combat flood and drought.

part of India while some other parts face drought. This drought-flood phenomenon is a recurring feature. One major part of the water mission would be networking of our rivers." The interlinking of rivers gained further importance in political, legislative and civil domains after the Supreme Court, order on October 31, 2002, for the completion of the interlinking of rivers within 10 years.[74]

ILR plans to bring the drinking water facility to 101 districts and 5 metropolitan cities.[75] It is doubtful if the river link would be the solution, when there are possible local water source management systems such as local ponds, lakes and common wells. Safeguarding the lakes and ponds and constructing the check dams in the traditional way could solve almost 90% of our drinking water problems.[76] The purpose of this project was to maximize the availability of utilizing water and water resource development by transferring water from surplus basins to water deficit basins/regions by interlinking rivers.[77] The National perspective comprises of two components, namely, the peninsular Rivers Development and the Himalayan Rivers Development.[78]

The point here is that if such projects do not find solutions for the existing problems they need to be critically looked at. This proposed project of linking all rivers through super dams and canals, as Vandana Shiva says, "Offers new opportunities for privatization, but entails cruelly heavy costs for our rivers and people. It will displace more than five million people, and ecosystems, people and communities will be deprived of water, which will be imprisoned by giant dams and canals of cement. This is a nightmare of slavery, a recipe for the extinction of a species and culture."[79]

---

74 Carolin Arul, *Water Laws and Rights in India* (Delhi: ISPCK & Chennai: UELCI, 2005), 148.

75 Suresh Prabhu, "Interlinking Problems" on River Linking, *The Hindu* (11.08. 2003), cited by Christopher Rajkumar, "Inclusive Need for Interlinking of Rivers," *Inclusive Growth in Globalised India: Challenges and Options*, edited by Jagadish Gandhi (New Delhi: Deep & Deep Publications, 2008), 249.

76 Christopher Rajkumar, *Ibid.*

77 Carolin Arul, *Water Laws and Rights in India*, 152.

78 *Ibid.*, 154. For a detailed description of these components see pp.154-158.

79 Vandana Shiva, *Globalization's New wars: Seed, Water and Life Forms* (New Delhi: Women Unlimited, 2005), 83.

Therefore, though this project had a vision, it could not look at these issues which could become the consequences of the project. Thus, it will create the social issues like, environmental concerns, displacement of people, doubtful drought resistance and flood control, ecological impact and other related issues. Hence, this cannot be a solution to the problem of water scarcity and drinking water.

2.2.12. Dam Constructions

Constructing large dams across the rivers in India is another issue that has to be given focus. As Ramaswamy R. Iyer says, "India has a long history of water management."[80] It was before the advent of the British rule there were small and local level structured systems to manage water in community level.[81] The dams were built with the primary reason that there are wide variations in the availability of water in the country. These variations led to proposals for the storing of river waters in reservoirs behind large dams: a) for transferring water from the season of abundance to that of scarcity, and b) for a long-distance water transfers from 'surplus' areas to water-short areas. The objective of flood moderation has also led to some dam-building.[82] Some of the above discussed water conflicts are related to this aspect of dams and reservoirs. In India, at present, the Sardar Sarovar Project on the Narmada in Gujarat State has been the centre of fierce controversy. The issue here is that the native tribals who were the community-owners of the locale water resources, who had been using water for agriculture for a long time, are, now, driven away. In the name of 'development' these common people have to lose their land, water

---

80 Ramaswamy R. Iyer, *Water: Perspectives, Issues, Concerns* (New Delhi: Sage Publications, 2003), 123.

81 Iyer further reports that, "all these (systems) changed with the advent of British rule and of 'modernity.' Control over water resources passed from the hands of the community into those of the state. While the ownership of natural resources was claimed by the state, their management passed into the hands of engineers and bureaucrats. The induction of Western engineering ushered in the era of large dams and there was a concomitant decline of traditional forms of small-scale, local, community-managed systems. The new projects became symbols of 'development'" (*Ibid.*).

82 See Ramaswamy R. Iyer, *Water: Perspectives, Issues, Concerns*, 123-124.

and the whole livelihood. The anti-dam movement like, Narmada Bachao Andolan (NBA) still fight for justice for the people.

2.2.13. Privatization of Water

Privatization of water sources is a phenomenon that is becoming increasingly popular in our world today. In the 1970s and 80s, bottled drinking water in India was unheard of. Now, it seems that everyone in the country is drinking water from plastic bottles, and reusing the empty plastic bottles for carrying tap water rather than consuming bottled water on a regular basis.

Due to the adoption of the neo-liberal economic ideology in the process of economic globalization, treatment of water as a "social good" has changed into a "commodity." As economic globalization creates and responds to an increasing demand for economic growth that can only be met by an expansion of markets, privatization created new markets, such as market of water.[83] Targeting the "water market" of other countries, especially in large cities of developing countries, became the new agenda of the big corporates.

In India, water utility companies like *Vivendi* and *Suez* of France[84] have entered the Indian market and are beginning to run water distribution systems. Such systems would provide water to those who can afford the market prices, and those that cannot, are out of providence. It is clear that the private sector companies have organized to make profit, and not to fulfill socially responsible objectives such as achieving universal access to water and sanitation.[85] When these are privatized, majority of people, particularly in pauperized countries have disastrous consequences.[86] Clearly, there will be more losers in a country like India than those who stand to

83 Martin Robra, "People's Struggle for Life are a source of inspiration for an enriching Spirituality," *National Council of Churches Review* CXXII/1 (January – February 2002), 4-5.

84 The largest of the European companies are the French multinational companies such as *Vivendi Universal* and *Suez*. These were urged to include water provision in the negotiation strategy.

85 Angela Saini, "Scarce 'blue gold'," 37.

86 Ulrich Duchrow, "Private Property: A Growing Danger for life (or: Neglected in the Globalization Debate)" *Ecumenical Review* 54/4 (October 2002), 478.

gain from such a system. The issue of privatization of water will be dealt with in detail in the next chapter.

Conclusion

Freshwater is emerging as one of the most critical natural resource issues facing humanity. Beyond the impact of population growth itself, the demand for freshwater has been rising in response to industrial development, increased reliance on irrigated agriculture, massive urbanization, and rising living standards. In this century, while world population has tripled, water withdrawals have increased by over six times. Moreover, the supply of freshwater available to humanity is shrinking, in effect, because many freshwater resources have become increasingly polluted. The rivers and other water resources have become receptacles for a degraded collection of wastes from municipal sewage, toxic industrial effluents, and harmful chemicals and ground water from agricultural activities.

The measures to defend drinking water, though they are set in the form of rights and policies, they have to be re-viewed and rephrased from a common citizen's outlook. Today, however, as Bharat Dogra comments, "the crisis of water scarcity that exists in vast areas of the country is a human-made crisis from various point of view, and it is not helpful to hide this fact behind pretexts of rain-failure. This has always been a part of life but the question is how best we can cope with it."[87] Therefore, it is not only a common human's responsibility rather it is also in the hands of the state and central governments to take precautionary measures to reduce, avoid, and get rid of these issues related to water and let every one to use water prudently.

---

87 Bharat Dogra, "Water Crisis Manmade," *Environment Protection Challenges and Issues: Impact of Rapid Development and Policy measures*, edited by V.S. Mahajan (New Delhi: Deep & Deep Publications, 1993), 114.

Chapter 3

"Water of Life" as Cornerstone for Theological Critique on Privatization of Drinking Water in India

Introduction

Water is an essential element for life. It is even more fundamental than food, for without it there is no food and while we can survive for some time without food, we cannot survive without water. Many people still confront daily the situation of an inadequate supply of safe water and the very serious resulting consequences. In many countries, agricultural activities are a major source of livelihood and an essential dimension of local social cohesion and culture. This activity is carried on by small farmers in rural areas, very often with huge constraints. However, it must be remembered that, in the end, the dominant use of water around the world will continue to be water for food security. Having discussed about the religious significance of water and water-related issues in the previous chapters let us probe into the possibilities to make theological critique on privatization of water with "water of life" as its basis within the umbrella of ecology.

3.1. Drinking Water

A worldwide crisis over water is brewing. According to the United Nations, 31 countries are now facing water scarcity and 1 billion people lack access to clean drinking water. Water consumption is doubling every 20 years and yet at the same time, water sources are rapidly being polluted, depleted, diverted and exploited for corporate interests ranging from industrial agriculture and manufacturing to electricity production and mining. It is predicted that by 2025, two-thirds of the world's population will suffer from lack of clean and safe drinking water.[1]

The centrality of freshwater in our lives cannot be overestimated. Lack of access to water for meeting basic needs such as health, hygiene and food security undermines development and inflicts enormous hardship on more than a billion members of the human family.[2] In the Millennium Declaration adopted by the United Nations' General Assembly in 2000, world leaders resolved 'to halve, by the year 2015, the proportion of the world's people who are unable to reach, or to afford, safe drinking water', and 'to stop the unsustainable exploitation of water resources'.[3] Drinking water is to satisfy the thirst of all creatures. Therefore, the quest here is to make critique on the evil forces which does not allow the creatures, including humans, to satisfy their thirst.

3.2. Privatization

Privatization is often assumed to entail commercialization and commodification, to the extent that the terms are, at times, used interchangeably. Privatization requires change of ownership, or

1 http://www.citizen.org/cmep/Water/general accessed on 12/09/2008.

2 Kofi Annan, "Forward," *Water for People: Water for Life* (United Nations World Water Development Report) (New York: UNESCO & Berghahn Books, 2003), XIX.

3 *Ibid.*

handover of management, from the public to the private sector.[4] Privatization is the *accumulation* of property and ownership of the right to *exclude* other from using it.[5] Furthermore, the term privatization could be interpreted as the process that involves the participation of private companies in the distribution and maintenance of public services with the government infrastructure at various levels of agreement and not necessarily controlling the assets.[6] It is an independent ownership and control. It includes all decision-making units that are not part of the government. The hallmark of the private sector is its response to the signals contained in the prices it pays for the resources it uses and the prices it can charge for the goods it produces.[7]

3.3. Privatization of Water: An Overview

Though we have discussed this briefly in the last chapter, my intention here is to get into deeper understanding of this phenomenon. The attitude towards water as an economic entity has led the private sector to cash in on the need for safe drinking water. The community, which has the economic potential, makes use of this privilege and the low-income category is left to the mercy of governments.[8] Governments entrust the private companies to secure the water resources and distribute it to the public. There were efforts to enhance the government policy to accommodate this process.[9] Apart from paying a fee to the government, the private companies would

---

4 Karen Bakker, *Neo-liberalising Nature? Market Environmentalism in Water Supply in England and Wales*, http://www.geog.ubc.ca/~bakker/PDF/neoliberalising.pdf, 544, cited by Anderson H.M. Jeremiah, "Privatization of Water - A Theological Critique and Ensuing Challenges for the Church," *Reformed World* 57/1 (March 2007), 4.

5 Kathryn Tanner, *Economy of Grace* (Minneapolis: Fortress Press, 2005), 34, cited by *Ibid.*

6 Anderson H.M. Jeremiah, "Privatization of Water ...," 4.

7 William J. Weida, "A General Economic Critique of Water Privatization," http://www.totse.com/en/politics/green_planet/164793.html accessed on 12/09/2008.

8 Anderson H. M. Jeremiah, "Privatization of Water ...," 4.

9 *Ibid.*, 5.

earn a huge profit by selling water to the public. Thus, privatization looks 'water as a commodity,' 'water as an economic good,' and 'water as a commercial product,' which is against the common heritage of water.

As we have discussed earlier, the new agenda of the big corporate became targeting the "water market" of other countries, especially in large cities of developing countries. The discussions of the related schemes and their strategies seem alarming. One of the World Bank discussions reflecting on the above schemes notes, "The water business needs to be made more attractive to gain more investment and to draw and retain new actors. Risk has to be rebalanced between the public and private sectors..."[10] Therefore, we have to make it clear that when private companies interfere in a country's economy, they, in fact, buy democracy for money. The whole idea of a corporation is to make profit, and profit only is its concern and not ensuring sustainability or equal access to water.

There are some countries, which realized that they are affected and they became great examples to see how the aftermath will be.[11] In India, though there are experiences of privatization of water already realized in many places, the formulated National Water Policies of 1987 and 2002 do not speak anything about privatization explicitly. But, they encourage the private sector to participate in water management.[12] Instead of protecting the water resources from self-interested profiteers, governments are retreating from

---

10 *Bread for the World*, "Water is a Human Right: Stop Commodification Now!," *Germany*, January 2004, p.5, cited by Solomon Victus, "Water – A Privatised Commodity…," 5-6.

11 Indian groups cite water projects controlled by Bechtel in Bolivia and the Philippines as examples of what India should avoid. Bechtel took over the water supply in Cochabamba city, Bolivia, in end-1999. In the space of a few months the price of drinking water had risen by two and a half time. The reason was a government guarantees to the powerful water firm that user fees would remain the same in dollars, so every time the local currency fell the price would spiral. By January 2000, an aggrieved population had taken to the streets demanding the privatization deal be cancelled. The government had no choice but to give in, although Bechtel now threatens it with a $25 million legal battle for breach of contract.

12 Solomon Victus, "Water – A Privatised Commodity…," 8-9.

their responsibilities and bending to the will of giant transnational corporations that are poised to profit from the shortage of water.[13]

We need to be cognizant that we can at a pinch do without certain industrial goods (such as soap, steel, fertilizer, etc.) or look for substitutes but we cannot do without water and there are no substitutes for it. We cannot reduce our intake of water (for drinking, cooking and washing) below a certain level. The supply cannot be allowed to fail.[14] Hence, it needs to be affirmed that water belongs to everybody.

3.4. Privatization of Water in India

3.4.1. Two levels of Privatization

In India, privatization of water could be seen in two levels, one in small-scale and the other in large-scale.

A) ***Small-scale privatization – domestic and local commercialization of water:***[15] The city of Chennai could be a case of this kind. As Anderson Jeremiah reports, "Chennai is one of the country's water starved cities. It depends for its water needs to a large extent on the dwindling ground water. With the heat and humidity, water consumption is very high. Exploiting this situation, more than 200 legal and 400 illegal water packaging units have spring up, utilizing the bore well water on their own small lands to meet the needs."[16] Perceiving the profitability of this market, bigger players like Nestle, Parle, Aquafina (Pepsi) and Kinley (Coco-Cola) have invested heavily and even brought out some of the smaller companies. Moreover, continuing failure of the municipal water distribution system promises a good future for these

13 http://www.citizen.org/cmep/Water/articles.cfm?ID=10842 accessed on 12.09.2008.

14 Ramaswamy R. Iyer, *Towards Water Wisdom*, 140.

15 Anderson H. M. Jeremiah, "Privatization of Water ...," 7.

16 *Ibid.*

companies and indirectly promotes and encourages private water vendors.[17]

B) ***Large-scale industrial and multinational takeover of water distribution and maintenance:***[18] Some of the archetypal mega projects of the modern markets could be traced here. The water distribution system in New Delhi, following the privatization of electricity, has been handed over to Vivendi and Degremont; the latter is in the process of design, build and distribute system in Sonia Vihar, New Delhi.[19] Another one in Tirupur, an industrial town chosen by the state government of Tamil Nadu to experiment a private build, operate, own and transfer model. This project was given to Bechtel and other Indian companies which have formed a consortium.[20] Apart from these, there are Coco-Cola and Pepsi establishments around the country involved in monopolizing water sources and causing severe ecological destruction.

3.4.2. Corollaries of Privatization of Water

Privatization of water eventually leads to various corollaries. Though they are interrelated they can be categorized as follows:

3.4.2.1. Economic consequences

a) ***Income disparity:*** In recent years, scarcity has turned water from an abundant resource to an expensive commodity. Forced upon poor and rich, consumers and industrial producers, similar rates for water use will also result in greater income disparity and deeper social cleavages, leading to higher risks of social disorder.[21] The

17 Anderson H. M. Jeremiah, "Privatization of Water ...," 7.

18 *Ibid.*

19 Anitha Sampath, et al., *Water Privatization and Implications in India*, http://studentorgs.utexas.edu/aidaustin/water/water _privatization.pdf., 6, cited by Anderson H.M. Jeremiah, "Privatization of Water ...," 7.

20 *Ibid.*

21 Solomon Victus, "Water – A Privatised Commodity...," 13.

price of privatized water involves the cost of purification, upgradation and distribution.[22] As water, thus, becomes more expensive it is unaffordable to the poor and they will be forced to seek alternative source of water from unreached well water and water from sewage ridden urban rivers.[23]

b) ***Lack of electricity:*** due to scarcity of water the generation of electricity became less and it leads to drastic power cuts. This disturbs the daily life of the people.

3.4.2.2. Social Consequences

The immediate consequences of the privatization of water are faced by the ones who live in the lower strata in our society, such as, Dalits, Tribals, women and children. Privatization reduces accessibility (less accessibility) to water. The most and immediate impact of reducing the accessibility and affordability of water falls on women and children. More people die due to the illness caused by drinking poor quality water.[24] However, the poor are denied of access to clean drinking water. Vandana Shiva calls this denial of poor people access to water by privatizing water distribution as terrorism.[25]

a) ***Elimination of public control:*** Privatization leads to the formation of water monopolies and thereby it eliminates public control over this resource.[26]

3.4.2.3. Ecological consequences

a) ***Depletion of ground water:*** Ground water is the primary source of drinking (fresh) water. A great majority of rural dwellers' land irrigated with ground water tends to be far more productive than the land irrigated with

22 Anderson H. M. Jeremiah, "Privatization of Water …," 8.

23 *Ibid.*

24 Coline Tan, "Water Crisis: Analysis and Proposals," *Third World Resurgence, Penage,* Nos.143-144, 8, cited by Solomon Victus, "Water – A Privatised Commodity…," 13.

25 Vandana Shiva, *Water Wars: Privatization, Pollution, and Profit,* xiv.

26 Anderson H.M. Jeremiah, "Privatization of Water …," 8.

dam-canal water. But, the control of water by TNCs (Transnational Corporations) and its involvement in the heavy consumption of underground water led to groundwater depletion from 15 feet to 40 feet.[27] They use high power compressors to suck water from the inner layer of the earth. Thus, unsustainable and uncontrolled water mining, with profit as the only motive, leads to an alarming fall in the ground water level[28] and destruction of groundwater source, which may cause saltwater intrusion and will damage the source of drinking water.

On the one side, when water is extracted by private companies it leads to drought on the other side, which affects not only human beings but also animals, plants and other creatures. In turn, it directs to ecological imbalance.

b) ***Global warming:*** the increase in temperature or climate change leads to the tendency to consume more water. Privatization would cause lack of availability of water.

3.4.2.4. Health Related Consequences

In the absence of the legal implementation of quality control, individuals and companies driven by profit compromise on water quality, thereby causes a serious threat to public health.[29] People living in *villas* (slums), for instance, have no access to fresh water. Digging a bore well is expensive and underground water is often polluted. Bottled water is expensive. Even those who pay for water cannot be sure if the water provided by the privatized company is safe. For example, the quality of water out-flowing from factories may have some toxic chemicals (including mercury). Though it is not used in the factories the arsenic may come from the pipeline.[30]

---

27 John Mohan Razu, "Water for People, Water for Life: An Ethical (Christian) Response," 33.

28 Anderson H.M. Jeremiah, "Privatization of Water …," 8.

29 *Ibid.*

30 Astrid Hardtke, "Privatizing God's Treasure for the World," 48.

3.4.3. Bottled Water: A Moral Issue

The effects of privatization of water are not only to be found in the large rivers and water bodies that are 'owned' by private corporations but are also to be found in the commercialization of water, in bottled water and aerated soft drinks. Both processes remove water from the control of people and communities and place it in the hands of profit making organizations.[31] The theological and ethical critique needs to be rooted in the notion that clean drinking water, like air, is a God-given resource that should not be packaged and sold. By quoting Cassandra Carmichael,[32] Rebecca U. Cho says that, "In the developing world, water is being sold as a commodity where the resource is scarce. On the rationale that bottling water takes water resources away from the poor, the environmental issue has become an important one for people of faith."[33] Therefore, the moral call has to be "water should not to be privatized and water should be free for all."

Though some of the bottled water companies began to comment on the issue of water positively, we need to unmask the false promises made by these kinds of corporate groups. Lisa Manley, the spokesperson of the Coca-Cola Company, said, "the company as a leading provider of bottled water with its *Dasani* brand, recognizes the serious nature of water issues and is working on several community initiatives in developing countries."[34] The recently modified label of bottled drinking water called *Aquafina*, the product of PEPSICO,[35] has a description about water under a caption "Replenish and Restore Our Water." It says thus:

---

31 Philip Vinod Peacock, "Water Conflict," *Waters of Life and Death: Ethical and Theological Responses to Contemporary Water Crises*, edited by Sam Peedikayil Mathew & Chandran Paul Martin (Delhi: ISPCK & Chennai: UELCI, 2005), 60.

32 She is the director of eco-justice programs for the National Council of Churches in USA.

33 Rebecca U. Cho, "Is bottled water a moral issue?," *CHRISTIAN CENTURY* (January 9,2007), 13.

34 *Ibid.*, 14.

35 This PEPSICO India Holdings Pvt. Ltd. Company situated in Kanjicode, East of Palakkad in Kerala.

> *"Water is mankind's most precious resource. At PepsiCo India, we are committed to give back to nature the water we use in our plants. Over the last two years, we have reduced our water consumption by recycling efficiently. This has helped us to save over 2 billion litres of water. We have also recharged over 40% of the water we consume through roof water harvesting and surface water ponds. By 2009, we target to achieve 'Zero Water Balance' with these initiatives. Come, partner with us in our effort to use water wisely, so that it can be enjoyed by our future generations."*

These neo-liberal creeds have to be tested and the untruths have to be exposed to the poor public of the developing countries and water should be made safe and accessible to all people.

Moreover, it is quite alarming that bottled waters have pesticide contents within them. Sathis Kumar and Ramaswamy report that, "A study conducted by the Center for Science and Environment, New Delhi, showed that most brands of bottled water were pesticide-laden. To meet this situation, the government appointed a committee on pesticide residue in packaged mineral water under the chairmanship of Dr. Satwant Reddy, and the committee suggested certain policy and regulatory measures."[36] Further, they note that the packaged mineral water multi-nationals are depleting water resources and lowering the groundwater table precariously, mainly for the purpose of accumulation of wealth and capital.[37] Thus, it has to be made aware theologically, that, as K.C. Abraham says, "The natural resources are unjustly exploited."[38] When he says 'the natural resources' it certainly includes water also. When water functions as an agent for justice and community building within the Bible, water is not satisfied unless justice is done. Thus, justice, being part of the Biblical vision, is denied to water.

---

36 G. Sathis Kumar and S. Ramaswamy, "Water for Sustainable Livelihood: Principles and Challenges," *Vikas Vani Journal* II/2 (April-June 2008), 63.

37 *Ibid.*

38 K. C. Abraham, *Transforming Vision: Theological – Methodological Paradigm Shifts* (Tiruvalla: Christava Sahitya Samithi, 2006), 119.

3.4.4. Why Oppose Privatization of Water?

Water privatization schemes throughout the world have a track record of skyrocketing prices, water quality problems, deteriorating service and a loss of local control. Privatization advocates argue – usually without any supporting evidence – that switching from publicly owned and operated utilities to private sector firms will lead to greater economic efficiency, stabilized rates, reduced public debt and improved budgetary management. In reality, privatization more often not fulfills any of these promises, and instead creates a number of new problems. Vulnerable to corruption and operating according to a profit-driven corporate agenda fundamentally incompatible with delivering an essential service, private water companies are failing to provide citizens with safe & affordable water. Private corporations seek to increase profit margins by cutting costs; hence privatization is almost always accompanied by lay-offs.[39]

India Centre for Human Rights and Law based in Mumbai states some reasons of opposing privatization of water. They are:[40]

a) It leads to increase in rates of water;
b) Privatization could undermine water quality;
c) Water companies are accountable to its shareholders and not the consumers;
d) Privatization fosters corruption;
e) Privatization reduces local control and public rights;
f) Private financing costs more than government financing;
g) Privatization leads to loss of jobs;
h) Privatization is difficult to reverse.

The multinational water corporations, their government allies, the IMF, the World Bank and the regional development banks have claimed that water privatization (or public/private partnerships) is the answer. They claim that bringing the private sector into water and sanitation service provision will ensure access to the more than

39 http://www.citizen.org/cmep/Water/articles.cfm?ID=10842 accessed on 12/09/2008.

40 *Environment Ambassador* (A Newspaper for Exnora International), 3/4 (April 2006), 6.

a billion people worldwide who lack clean and affordable water, and the 2.4 billion who lack sanitation services. The water corporations and their allies argue that the private sector is more efficient, cost-effective and competitive. And, the private sector can bring needed financing.[41] These kind of false promises are made by privatization, which cannot be worked out in a country like, India. Therefore, on the above discussed grounds, privatization of water has to be resisted.

3.5. Theological Critique on Privatization of Water

Water is the most abundant resource that God has given to humankind and other life forms but now a precious commodity. All living beings, big and small, sustain life with water. Therefore, a theological reflection must be concerned with issues relevant to our daily struggles, both as individuals and humanity. In general, it is the task of theology to provide us with the stimulation to act and direct our actions towards the fulfillment of life and human dignity for all.[42] There is plurality of theologies. It arises from different contexts. As Miroslav Volf puts it, "the plurality of social worlds is reflected in an increasing plurality of theologies."[43] Amidst of the plurality of theologies, we can apply appropriate theological thoughts in order to substantiate the critique on privatization of water. This would lead us to have apt, credible, and action-oriented reflection on water with regard to life.

41 *Environment Ambassador* (A News Paper for Exnora International), 3/4 (April 2006), 6.

42 Atle Sommerfeldt, "Forward" in *Waters of Life and Death: Ethical and Theological Responses to Contemporary Water Crises,* edited by Sam P. Mathew and Chandran Paul Martin (Chennai: UELCI & Delhi: ISPCK), ix.

43 Miroslav Volf, "A Queen and a Beggar: Challenges and Prospects of Theology," (Introduction) *The Future of Theology: Essays in Honor of Jurgen Moltmann,* edited by Miroslav Volf, Carmen Krieg and Thomas Kucharz (Grand Rapids, Michigan: William B. Eerdmans Publishing Company, 1996), x.

3.5.1. Various Theological Affirmations on Water

3.5.1.1. Patristic Theology

Tertullian, in his treatise, *De Baptisma*, affirms the creative capacity of water in Genesis. It says thus:

> *"O man, you should have reverence for the antiquity of the waters as a primordial element. It was in the midst of the water that the earth appeared: once the elements of the world were set in order, when it was to be given inhabitants, it was the primordial waters which were commanded to produce living creatures...the primordial water brought forth life, so that no one should be astonished that in Baptism the waters are able to give life."*[44]

St. Cyril of Jerusalem, in his catechetical lectures refers the connection of the primordial water and the Baptismal water. He writes:

> *"If you wish to know why it is by means of water and not some other elements that grace is given, you will find the reason in going through the scriptures. Water is a wonderful thing and the most beautiful of the four sensible elements of the cosmos – the sky is the dwelling of the angels but the skies are made of water; earth is the home of men (sic.), but the earth has come out of the waters; and before the creation of visible things in six days, the spirit of God hovered over the waters. The water is the principle of the cosmos and the Jordan of the Gospel."*[45]

---

44 Tertullian, "On Baptism," *The Anti Nicene Fathers Vol.III*, edited by Alexander Roberts and James Donaldson (Grand Rapids, Michigan: William B. Eerdman, 1957), 670, cited by Joji K. Joy, "Symbolism of Water in the West Syrian Liturgy: An Interpretation from Biblical and Patristic Perspectives and Its Implication in the Modern Context" (M.Th. Thesis, Senate of Serampore College, 1999), 55.

45 St. Cyril of Jerusalem, "On Baptism," *Nicene and Post Nicene Fathers, Vol. VIII*, edited by Philip Schaff and Henry Wace (Grand Rapids, Michigan: William B. Eerdman, 1955), 118, cited by Joji K. Joy, "Symbolism of Water in the West Syrian Liturgy...," 55.

As these examples say, patristic writings give emphasis to water and its significance in the life of creatures is affirmed.

3.5.1.2. Process Theology

Process theology contributes to environmental ethics where it says that human and non-human lives are not separated and therefore the idea of interdependence is affirmed. A.N. Whitehead, who developed process theology, extends the idea that biological world is a web of mutual dependencies as "an ecological view of reality."[46] Process thought leads to an emphasis on divine immanence in nature and it encourages respect for nature.[47] Therefore, in this sense, it also urges us to respect water resources as well. In relation to ecotheology, process thought advocates *kenosis* or self-emptying.

A Paradigm of Kenotic Anthropocentrism: A call for *kenotic anthropocentrism* can be seen in process theology. This is modeled on Christ who emptied himself of all his 'dominion.' This word is used to denote his humility and service, not the mastery over others, even the mastery over water resources. Thus, this model should lead us to get rid of mastery mind over nature and to have service-mindedness. That is, Christ as the *Dominus*[48] should be our model for our entire understanding of human dominion over nature and this sets the paradigm for a Christian approach to creation. Thus, *kenosis* has a specific 'eco-just' implication.[49]

3.5.1.3. Theology of the Sacraments

Water, both as metaphor and reality, is a major theme in the sacrament, which focuses on water and baptism but is more

---

46 Ian G. Barbour, *Religion and Science: Historical and Contemporary Issues* (New York: Harper Collins Publishers, 1997), 285.

47 *Ibid.*, 291.

48 *Dominus* is of the Latin origin used to denote 'dominion,' which is the root word used to refer to the 'lordship' of Christ who demonstrated his dominion in humility and service, i.e., as a servant.

49 See George Mathew Nalunnakkal, *Green Liberation: Towards an Integral Ecotheology* (Delhi: ISPCK/NCCI, 1999), 261-264.

concerned with cleansing than with water's necessity for survival.[50] In baptism, water is given importance as element that cleanses the old evil natures and gives a new life. Rather than washing and pouring, *bathing* is mentioned to have full cleansing. Baptism is the bath that plunges one into the "name of Jesus" (1Cor.1:13). Among different meanings, one meaning indicates that, "the elements served in the Eucharist – the bread and wine – are the fruits of the earth and of human labour"[51] whereby water, which is used for mixing with wine, falls into the fruits of the earth. Here, these are presented to God, the Creator in faith and thanksgiving for the blessings/fruits of the earth. "In certain parts of the world, where bread and wine are not customary or obtainable, it is now sometimes held that local food and drink serve better to anchor the Eucharist in everyday life."[52] Therefore, water could also, if needed, to be served in the place of wine, which could signify the importance of water. Thus, theological reflections of sacraments keep significant place for water.

3.5.1.4. Eco-theology[53]

When 'ecology' became a significant theological category, the theological reflection highlighted on the eco-centric life thereby it is called as eco-theology. Among the four levels of ecology,[54] both

---

50 Timothy Gorringe, *Harvest: Food, Farming and the Churches* (London: SPCK, 2006), 75.

51 William H. Lazareth and Nikos Nissiotis, *Baptism, Eucharist and Ministry* (Faith and Order Paper no.111) (Geneva: WCC, 1982), 10-11.

52 *Ibid.*, 17.

53 Eco-Theology is a part of the discipline of Christian Ethics. It deals with the Christian understanding of Nature and Creation, especially the Christian responsibility in safeguarding the natural environment. It is often called as "environmental theology" (Per Larsson, *"Your will be done on earth..." – Ecological Theology for Asia: An Ecumenical Textbook for Theological Schools* [Hong Kong, China: Christian Conference of Asia, 2004], 24).

54 The four levels are: 1) *Environmental ecology*, which concerned with non-excessive disfigurement of environment and seeks to preserve the quality of life; 2) *Social ecology*, which considers not only the natural environment, but also human beings and society within nature; 3) *Mental ecology*, which holds that the causes of the earth's deterioration are not found simply in the kind of society and development we have at present, but also are rooted in our

environmental and social ecology call us for a theological quest with regard to water. Combined with the eco-ethical claims eco-theological reflections make a strong critique on the *domination* of human beings over the creation and calls for conservation of natural resources. On a thriving earth, human well-being is nurtured not only by the provision of an earth productive of sufficient food, with water fit for all to drink, air fit to breathe, forests kept replenished, renewable resources continuously renewed, non-renewable resources used sparingly but also by a way of living within the natural order that is fitting: respectful of the integrity of natural systems and of the worth non-human creatures.[55]

Here, by taking the situation of the natural resources, including water, into consideration, it proposed the model of "stewardship" in which humans are designated as stewards of the earth and its resources in order to save the earth and related resources. Humanity's higher responsibility to "till" and "keep," that is, to manage, to preserve and to protect the earth is demanded in this stewardship. Furthermore, as co-creators with God, human beings are expected to guide the earth's productivity and conserve its gifts. Therefore, it is clear that the domination over water and related resources is very much criticized in the eco-theological reflections.

3.5.1.5. Eco-feminism[56]

Ecology and feminism brought together in the unified perspective of eco-feminism and later it became a movement. The eco-feminist movement calls the women to lead an ecological revolution to save

---

mind-set today, whose roots extend from earlier periods into modern history; 4) *Holistic or integral ecology*, which takes as its starting point a new vision of earth. It sees the earth and human beings as a single entity. (Leonardo Boff, "Ecology," Dictionary of Third World Theologies, edited by Virginia Fabella and R.S. Sugirtharajah [Maryknoll, New York: Orbis Books, 2000], 80-82).

55 R. L. Sarkar, *The Bible, Ecology and Environment* (Delhi: ISPCK, 2000), 197.

56 The French writer Francoise d'Eaubonne coined the term *eco-feminisme* in 1974. Out of women's movement the eco-feminist movement emerged in the 1970s as a response to the increasing consciousness of the connections between women and their commitment to the protection of creation (Aruna Gnanadason, *Listen to the Women! Listen to the Earth!* [Geneva: WCC Publications, 2005], 31).

the planet. It was expected that such an ecological movement would entail new gender relations between women and men between humans and nature.[57] In eco-feminism, the aspect of 'Motherhood' of women is seen in par with the earth. As "Motherhood, in India, is a strong symbol of nurture and care,"[58] the nurturing and caring nature of the earth for the human life is affirmed. Moreover, in eco-feminist perspective, as Rebecca Sangeetha observes "water and women are perceived as interchangeable metaphors."[59] Her highlight on the "Fertility link" between water and women further adds more light on this discussion. She says, "Both women and water are considered to be sources of fertility because both enjoy the potential of procreation. Water is necessary for germination of seeds and for enhancing the fertility power of the soil and the woman is the primary source of new life."[60] But what happens here is that the patriarchal society or male controls this reproduction, for which feminism makes strong critique. Thus, eco-feminism also opposes the control over water and privatization of the primary source of life.

3.5.2. Biblical-Theological Critique

The Bible comes from an area where fertile valleys stand between deserts, and the threat of drought is common. Beginning from the creation stories to the life of Israelites for whom water became important, then to the prophets for whom fresh water is a key metaphor for a new age, then to the gospel of John where Jesus Christ is affirmed as the spring of living water and finally to the promise in Revelation that "to the thirsty I will give the water of life," the Bible respects and affirms water.[61] Likewise, theology, as David

---

57 Carolyn Merchant, *Earth Care: Women and the Environment* (New York: Routledge, 1995), 5, cited by Aruna Gnanadason, *Listen to the Women! Listen to the Earth!*, 31-32.

58 Aruna Gnanadason, *Listen to the Women! Listen to the Earth!*, 41.

59 D. Rebecca Sangeetha, "Genderization of Water," *Waters of Life and Death: Ethical and Theological Responses to Contemporary Water Crises*, edited by Sam P. Mathew & Chandran Paul Martin (Delhi: ISPCK & Chennai: UELCI, 2005), 122.

60 *Ibid.*

61 Timothy Gorringe, *Harvest: Food, Farming and the Churches*, 75-76.

Tracy emphasizes, "should play a role in the public realm because theology helps us all to ask the kind of questions which all reflective human beings ask. Like all the other liberal arts, like psychology and sociology, theology attempts to ask these questions in a disciplined way faithful to the canons of inquiry of modernity."[62] Moreover, Theology can be described as the attempt to establish, in both theory and practice, mutually critical correlations between two sets of interpretation: an interpretation of the Christian tradition and an interpretation of contemporary experience.[63] Hence, by coalescing these two, we need to make a critique from this biblical-theological perspective.

3.5.2.1. Water: Source of all Life

Water is, according to Mircea Eliade, the "reservoir of all the possibilities of existence."[64] It is pre-formal. Because of this special characteristic, it is through water that all form arises. In a real sense, water *is* the basis of life. It is vital for the very existence of plants, beasts and human beings, for their growth, nurture and increase.

3.5.2.2. Drinking Water: Life Sustaining and Nurturing Force

As humans, our bodies are mostly made up of water, and they require a constant flow of water through them for nourishment and waste removal. In a very real sense *we are what we drink*. Furthermore, every living being requires water. It takes only a little imagination to

62 David Tracy, "The Role of Theology in Public Life: Some Reflections," *Word and World* 4/3 (Summer 1984): 231-232. More exactly, in the wider public realm, theology can also serve as the interpretation of the religious classics of the culture for a given individual. The interpretation of the religious classics should be disclosive of those religious questions which human beings, as human beings, ask and provide critical reflection on the kinds of responses which the religious classics suggest (232).

63 *Ibid.*, 235. Furthermore, from Tracy's view, if the correlational model for theology is as sound as many of us have come to believe, then it not merely allows but demands that theology enter into serious conversation with all others in the public realm (234-235).

64 M. Eliade, *Le Sacré et le Profane*, 112, cited in Martha Franks, "The Need for a Theology of Water: the Drought of Spiritual Power in Environmental Law and Politics" (an unpublished paper), 1.

see that the water system which percolates and tunnels through Earth is analogous to our own circulation system which carries nourishing blood to all the organs of the body. Each of us began life in the waters of the womb; and our remains will eventually become one with Earth and its watery depths.[65]

Certain virtues of water undoubtedly make all lives possible. Water is *beneficial to all* as its primary virtue it benefits to all things. It benefits all without exception. There is no election or selection and there is no exclusion. Water goes everywhere. On the contrary, we see today's neo-liberal economic globalization benefits only a few. The majority of people are excluded from the benefits of the current dominant economic system.[66] In the same way *making life possible* is another virtue of water, which by flowing continually, makes the life of every part of the body possible. This is also expected from a country's economy that it should make life possible: if it does not, it needs to be reformed. But as we experience today's neo-liberal economy makes life impossible. Not only the majority of the world population but also all creatures, air, water, earth, forests, animals and so on are suffering with the current economic system, and their life is not possible. This needs to be reformed.[67]

---

65 Nancy Bloomer, "The Ever-Moving Life Force," *The Living Pulpit* (January-March 2005), 22.

66 Park Seong–Won, "Economy of Water: A Spiritual Basis for an Alternative Economy" *Ecumenical Review* 57/2 (April 2005), 174.

67 *Ibid.*, 177. There are other virtues of water such as: a) *Continual flow:* Here the very nature of water is to "keep flowing," at least when there is a need to flow. Water never stops flowing. When it does, it becomes polluted. It is, therefore, crucially important to let water flow. Running is the very nature of water. It should continue to flow, not be accumulated in the hands of a few, but reach every corner and all people in society. It is important to let water flow, and flow normally; b) *Stability and inclitowenedd:* The deeper the water is, the more it is stable. When there is enough saving of water, the stability is greater. The lack of depth in water means vulnerability. Thus saving is an important element for economic stability; c) *Benevolence:* Water is benevolent in that it gives itself. Water never keeps water for itself. Water exists for giving to others. "Giving" is the very nature of economy. If economy cannot give what is necessary for those in need, it is no longer economy (*Ibid.*, 174-175).

3.5.2.3. Ownership over Resources

3.5.2.3.1. The Principle of Common Heritage

With regard to the ownership of the resources we have to have a principle like that of *the principle of common heritage*. By advocating this principle, David C. Korten intends that we need to recognize that "the environmental resources of the planet are common heritage resources and it is that right of every person – present and future – to share them in their beneficial use. These cannot be rightfully monopolized or used in ways contrary to the broader interest of present and future generations."[68] This principle proposes a people and life-centered function rather than corporate centered. Therefore, the natural resources have to be shared for the common benefit of all, which includes all living creatures of the earth. Ulrich Duchrow opines the same that God has given the world to human beings in common and nobody has originally a private dominion. Therefore, we cannot justify the private appropriation of the earth and its resources.[69] Thus, in this sense, private ownership over the resources is not at all encouraged.

3.5.2.3.2. God as the Owner

The principle of public accountability is grounded in our answerability of God. God, the Creator and Lord, is the real owner and proprietor, the only One, whose right in the world is absolute.[70] This is biblically substantiated from Ps.24:1-2, where it says, "The earth is the Lord's and all that is in it, the world, and those who live in it; for he has founded it on the seas, and established it on the rivers."[71] In this sense, human beings are not owners but rather

68 David C. Korten, *When Corporations Rule the World* (USA: Kumarian Press and Barrett-Koehler Publishers, 1995), 273.

69 Ulrich Duchrow, "Private Property: A Growing Danger for life…," 473.

70 Thomas Sieger Derr, *Ecology and Human Liberation: A Theological Critique of the Use and Abuse of Our Birthright* (Geneva: World Council of Churches, 1973), 71.

71 This is from NRSV. There are other versions, which explain explicitly this verse. "The earth *is* the LORD's, and all its fullness, The world and those who dwell therein. For He has founded it upon the seas, And established it upon the waters" (NKJV). "The earth is the Lord's and all it holds, the world and those

God's appointed caretakers, or managers, or, in the New Testament metaphor, God's "stewards."[72] However, as I pointed out earlier, the accountability that human beings have is from the common heritage, on the resources, that is inherited from God.

Therefore, the obligations inherent in ownership would seem to make a case for the equal sharing of the natural resources of the earth. Thus, land, minerals, water rights, air rights, and the like is obviously subject to these moral restraints.[73]

3.5.2.4. Ownership of Water

In the creation account, in Genesis, it is apparent that God created *order* from *chaos* and directed water towards earth with a good and common purpose that all, human and non-human beings, would benefit from it equally. Furthermore, in the biblical references such as, Ps.78:13, 15, 16;[74] Ps.104: 10, 11;[75] and Ps.107:35[76] the psalmist rightfully claims, by referring to the act of God in the exodus event, that God is the owner and proprietor of water. Moreover, we see God, who is the owner of water resources, speak against and condemn Pharaoh, the king of Egypt who claimed that the river Nile is his own and he himself has made it (Ezek. 29). God calls him as a "great dragon."[77] In Lamentations 5:4, we see a cry of people of who pay for their drinking water – "*We must pay for the water we drink.*" God gave water as a free gift for the benefit of God's creation. Therefore,

---

who live there. For God founded it on the seas, established it over the rivers" (The New American Bible).

72 Thomas Sieger Derr, *Ecology and Human Liberation,* 71.

73 *Ibid.*, 75.

74 "He divided the sea and let them pass through it, and made the waters stand like a heap... He split rocks open in the wilderness, and gave them drink abundantly as from the deep. He made streams come out of the rock, and caused waters to flow down like rivers."

75 "You make springs gush forth in the valleys; they flow between the hills, giving drink to every wild animal; the wild asses quench their thirst."

76 "He turns a desert into pools of water, a parched land into springs of water."

77 Thus says the Lord God: I am against you, Pharaoh king of Egypt, the great dragon sprawling in the midst of its channels, saying, "My Nile is my own; I made it for myself" (Ezek.29:3).

no one, except God, has the right to privately own water. Privatizing water and related resources is usurping God's ownership on water. Water should not be misappropriated by vested interests and should not be subjected to the any form of domination and exploitation. Rather, as a gift of God, water must be shared among all of God's creation.

3.5.2.5. Privatization as 'Leviathan'

Privatization of water has to be resisted. To defy the repressions of privatization, I would propose to see privatization of water as 'Leviathan,' a mythological symbol that few writers of the Bible have extracted from the ancient myths.[78] Though there are many scholars who explain what a myth is, I would opt for the definition proposed by Gerald A. Arbuckle, who defines myth as "a story or tradition that claims to reveal, in an imaginative or symbolic way, a fundamental truth about the world and human life. This truth is regarded as authoritative by those who accept it."[79] Leviathan, as the author of

78 The background for this terminology is found in the ancient Near Eastern mythology of the ascendancy of the local deity to active headship of the pantheon by defeating the power of Chaos – represented by the dual picture of the raging Sea or a fearsome Dragon – at the creation of the ordered world. (John N. Day, "God and Leviathan in Isaiah 27:1," *Bibliotheca Sacra* 155 [October-December 1998], 425).

79 Gerald A. Arbuckle, *Earthing the Gospel: An Inculturation Handbook for the Pastoral Worker* (New York: Orbis, 1990), 35, quoted by Wendell D'Cruz, *A Warli-Christian Story: An Experiment in Story Theology* (New Delhi: ISPCK, 1999), 1. Also, as the term is used technically in theological discussion it seems to have four nuances any or all of which may be present at any one time. They are: 1) A myth may be story which attempts to explain the origin of things without the use of modern historical and scientific investigation. Myth can thus be represented as pre-scientific thinking and this may lead to negative evaluation of it; 2) A Myth may depict some aspect of human experience in the form of a story about the past. The story of an original 'social contract' which expresses the structure of the society by a fiction's example of how it began would be a myth of this kind; 3) A myth may be story which is presented in terms of some symbolism and thus has a poetic or emotional appeal and is capable of reinterpretation in the light of fresh experiences. Some of the deepest feelings of people about the human predicament may find expression in mythological form [See I. H. Marshall, "Myth," *New Dictionary of Theology*, edited by Sinclain B. Ferguson and David F. Wright (Illinois: Inter-varsity

Job describes, is a sea monster exemplifying the fierce nature. In the Bible there are references that talk about Leviathan to convey the meaning of "evil power." In Isaiah 27:1, it is referred as "the Ancient Serpent," "the Crooked Serpent," "the sea Dragon," for which the punishment of Yahweh's sword will be hard, great, and strong and God will kill that which is in the Sea. Gregory Wayne Parsons sees the Leviathan as primarily referring to the crocodile, but asserts that it "is described in poetic hyperbole and even in mythopoeic language in order to heighten its role as a symbol of cosmic evil."[80] It is also explained in the same verse that Leviathan is a gliding and coiling serpent of the sea, which, with its twisting nature, creates caricaturing in the regularity.

In the context of scriptural passages that extol Yahweh for Yahweh's creative acts, mention is often made of Yahweh's victory over sea and dragon in language strikingly reminiscent of the Canaanite myth. Primary among these is Job 26:7-14. Although the term "Leviathan" is not present in that passage, synonymous designations are seen there. But Job 3:8 does use the term, and does so in reference to the Chaos monster.[81] Here Leviathan is a force of

---

Press, 1988), 449-451]. Though in the modern Western world myth is largely a foreign concept, it was the native vehicle of the ancients, through which they sought both to understand and to express the deep mysteries of life. As such, "myth in its purest form is concerned with 'primordial events' and seeks static structures of meaning behind or beyond the historical flux" [Frank Moore Cross, *Canaanite Myth and Hebrew Epic: Essays in the History of the Religion of Israel* (Cambridge, MA: Harvard University Press, 1973), viii].

80 Gregory Wayne Parsons, "A Biblical Theology of Job 38: 1-42: 6" [Th. D. diss., Dallas Theological Seminary, 1980], 345, cited by John N. Day, "God and Leviathan in Isaiah 27:1," 429.

81 John N. Day, "God and Leviathan in Isaiah 27:1," *Bibliotheca Sacra* 155 (October-December 1998), 429. The most extended treatment of Leviathan in the Bible is found in association with Behemoth in Job 40-41 Their description, in contrast to the prevailing treatment, is given in what appears to be a combination of both animaban (hippopotamus and crocodile) and mythological traits. Day believes that Behemoth and Leviathan here are best understood as "chaos monsters subdued by Yahweh at the time of creation Just as Leviathan ultimately derives from the Ugaritic dragon *Itn,* so Behemoth has its origin in an ox-like creature of the water called *Ars* or 'El's calf Atik, who is twice actually mentioned alongside the dragon *Itn* in the Ugaritic

"darkness" (3:8) and cannot be defeated by man (chapter 40). In the creation account we see "God separated between the light and the darkness." This, in more literal language, is what Job 26:7-13 described in mythic language – "that a hostile dragon symbolized that state of darkness and sea at the time of creation."[82] Here, "that state of darkness, confusion, and lifelessness is contrary to the nature of God in whom there is no darkness. God is called the God of light and life; the God of order."[83] It is also referred as the tyrant with the seven heads (Ps.74:14). It is a symbol of evil. However, we see the most terrifying of all creatures, the personification of chaos, is fully and finally destroyed by Yahweh.

Furthermore, Pharaoh, the monarch of Egypt who, in the Old Testament is presented as the enemy of God par excellence, as the most formidable human foe of God, is termed as "the sea monster" in poetic language: "Behold, I am against you, O Pharaoh king of

texts, and with whose defeat the deities Baal, Anat and Kothar-and-Hasis were associated" (John Day, *God's Conflict with the Dragon and the Sea* [Cambridge: Cambridge University Press, 1985], 86). Driver and Gray concur, viewing them as "mythical monsters described partly on the basis of mythological tradition, partly by means of traits derived from the hippopotamus and the crocodile" (Samuel Rolles Driver and George Buchanan Gray, *A Critical and Exegetical Commentary on the Book of Job,* International Critical Commentary [Edinburgh Clark, 1977], 352).

Wakeman notes that the "mythical allusions and the names are poetic hyperbole the distinctions between crocodile and mythical serpent cannot, in the nature of things, be firmly drawn" (Mary K. Wakeman, *God's Battle with the Monster: A Study in Biblical Imagery* [Leiden Brill, 1973], 65). And Gibson also concludes that, although it is not improbable that the poet was giving Leviathan some of the distinctive features of the crocodile, that does not affect the role Leviathan plays – the embodiment of cosmic evil, which is identical with that played by the Leviathan who had to be crushed by Yahweh at the beginning of time but who will not be finished off by Him until the end of time Job was presented with the real cause of his sufferings – the existence in Yahweh's world of an evil power that only Yahweh can control (J. C. L. Gibson, "A New Look at Job 41 1-4 (English 41 9-12)," *Text as Pretext Essays in Honor of Robert Davidson,* edited by Robert P. Carroll [Sheffield: JSOT, 1992], 130).

82 Bruce K. Waltke, *Creation and Chaos* (Portland, OR: Western Conservative Baptist Seminary, 1974), 58, cited by John N. Day, "God and Leviathan in Isaiah 27:1," 432.

83 *Ibid.*

Egypt, the great dragon sprawling in the midst of its channels, saying, "My Nile is my own; I made it for myself" (Ezek.29:3). The crooked nature of Pharaoh is compared with that of Leviathan.

Thus, we need to see privatization of water as the Leviathan that is becoming a cosmic evil. The attitudes that Leviathan has are replicated in the process of privatization. The corporations that privatize water are monstrous and gigantic evil powers, which seemingly swallow the water resources of the country. As Leviathan glides and coils, privatization of water twists the economy of India with its pseudo neoliberal creeds. Privatization of water is a force of darkness which forcefully pushes poor people into the state of darkness, confusion and lifelessness. Privatization of water is tyrant in nature because it oppresses the poor, including women and children, with its autocratic domination. With its leviathanic nature, in fact, it disrupts and creates turmoil in the regular flow of life. Moreover, Leviathan is a symbol of death. In this sense, privatization of water is also a symbol of death, which gradually swallows the life of common people by ingesting the water resources and leading them not towards life but death. From the words of God, the owner of water resources, who labeled Pharaoh, who claimed the ownership of the river Nile, as a great dragon, we can assert that privatization of water is the Leviathan in the country. We must resist this in order to overcome this evil power and defend our water resources.

3.5.2.6. Privatization is Neo-Colonialism

Colonialism has existed since the earliest times of human history, in different forms. Colonialism is not only a political and economic venture, but also a result of an individual's lust for power, the epitome of man's capacity for evil.[84] Under the banner of globalization and new-liberalism, India is now being colonized day by day. Privatization of water could be an apt example. Jayachitra, while discussing about postcolonial exploration of water, says that we need to challenge privatization for "we are already under the vices of neo-colonialism as we live under the economical hegemony of multinational

84 Rashmi Nair, "Modern Colonialism," *Water [sold] is Life, Right* (a pamphlet) (Bangalore: SCMI, n.d.), 7.

companies."[85] The multinational giants are invading the country, extracting the natural resources, modifying, and selling them in the same country and taking the profits back to their countries. Therefore, privatization of water is a modern colonialism for which the citizens are becoming subordinates.

3.5.2.7. Water represents God's Presence

Water, as life-source, symbolizes God's creative presence.[86] In the creation account, we see that the Spirit of God was hovering over the waters, which indicates the presence of God over the waters. The Israelites had much appreciation for the life-giving springs of fresh water. In their long journey through the desert the assurance of the presence of Yahweh is evident from the miraculous gift of water (Ps. 105:41). But the ultimate sign of the goodness of Yahweh is seen in bringing the people into the land of promise -"a land that has rivers and springs, and underground streams gushing out into the valleys and hills; a land that produces wheat and barley, grapes, figs, pomegranates, olives and honey" (Deut. 8:7) - the land of water![87] Wherever they had water there they felt the presence of Yahweh. Therefore, from the ecological doctrine of creation point, we need to assert the *immanence* of God that God, the Creator and the Spirit of the universe, still indwells among us through water.

3.5.2.8. Water of Life

This reflection is mostly of the relation of water with the aspects of life. 'Life' is a reality that has so many dimensions to it that has to be discussed from various angles.[88] 'Water' serves as an important

---

85 Jayachitra, "A Postcolonial Exploration of Water in the Fourth Gospel," *Bangalore Theological Forum* 37/2 (December 2005), 117.

86 Joseph A. Grassi, "Water," *The Collegevilla Pastoral Dictionary of Biblical Theology*, edited by (Bangalore: Theological Publications in India, 2005), 1060.

87 Wesley Ariarajah, "The Water of Life," *The Ecumenical Review* 34/3 (July 1982), 275.

88 M. M. Ross, "Water for Life, Water of Life and Water as Life: Meaning and Symbol in Theology," *Water Struggle*, edited by V. J. John (Kolkata: Bishop's College & Delhi: ISPCK), 85.

element for the life itself and at the same time points to God who is the foundation of all, that is, of life, water and of the human. By the virtue of its numerous uses it becomes a symbol or a paradigm. In the religious realm water is much associated with Christian tradition. Water can be a threat to creation (destructive waters). At the same time, in Baptism, water becomes a symbol of our reconstitution in divine action. Here, it is used in twofold meanings: water as that which drowns (and in the process totally removes sin) and water as that refreshes.[89] In the Old Testament, water, especially, spring water, had symbolized the life that God gave, particularly in the Messainic age.

Fresh, flowing water, also creating and maintaining life, in the Old Testament stood for divine activity and in quickening men (sic.) to life – as long as they did not forsake the Lord, the fountain of living water and go to 'leaky cisterns' (Jer.2:3). And wherever, the river flowed out of Jerusalem, everything would live (Exod. 47:9).[90] Also Jesus refers himself as the giver of 'living water,' which enabled the Samaritan woman to long for the gift of eternal life (Jn.4: 4-10).

Here, we ought to find both the physical and spiritual insight that water gives in our lives. Water, however, contains life in itself which becomes a life force to human and nonhuman beings. Thus, 'living water' gives life to all. As Nancy Bloomer says, "Living water means flowing water as opposed to water that is standing still. Flowing water is more healthful because moving water purifies itself and also picks up oxygen and nutrients for the life it contains."[91] Thus, water, though it is a colorless, odorless, tasteless substance made up of two hydrogen atoms and one oxygen atom, as an "ever-moving life force," is alive in and through our life.[92]

---

89 M. M. Ross, "Water for Life, Water of Life and Water as Life: Meaning and Symbol in Theology," *Water Struggle*, edited by V. J. John (Kolkata: Bishop's College & Delhi: ISPCK), 89.

90 Vandana, *Waters of Fire* (Madras: CLS, 1981), 50.

91 Nancy Bloomer, "The Ever-Moving Life Force," 22.

92 *Ibid.*

3.5.3. Water of Life is Theology of Life: Towards a Theology of Water

The physical necessity of water to every biosystem, human or non-human, means that the shortages of water that are increasing in the world, as well as the rising tides that may come as the earth warms, are crises for every community of creatures. Water, therefore, is both an essential symbol of the spirit, and also essential to physical life.[93]

In John's Gospel, Jesus is portrayed as 'life.' The same Jesus in the same Gospel says that He is the "living water," thus water becomes life and therefore, water is life. This concept can only be understood by the people who live in the context of scarce of water. Prophet Jeremiah describes God as *"the fountain of living Waters"* (Jeremiah 2:13; 17:13). And in John 4:14 Jesus says that "... *but those who drink of the water that I give them will never be thirsty. The water that I will give will become in them a spring of water gushing up to eternal life."* According to John the living water is water for life. This life-giving water will satisfy the thirst of the needy. And God-self is the only component who satisfies the thirsty one. So it is very easy for us to understand that God-self is water.[94]

The Bible also affirms "life" as a precious gift of God. It is clear from the Bible that we are not the creators or the owners of life, but God and God alone remains the source of life. When we understand the actual life situations we find that it has fallen short of what God intends for God's creation. Life itself in the planet earth is threatened by ecological disaster and nuclear threat. It is diminished by congenital deformities, violations of human rights and dignity, utter poverty, oppression, exploitation and so on.[95] Mohan Razu affirms that, "for theology, life is the starting point and the criterion is life, as God wanted it, created it, life in fullness, respect."[96] He further

93 Martha Franks, "The Need for a Theology of Water: the Drought of Spiritual Power in Environmental Law and Politics" (an unpublished paper), 1.

94 D. Moody Smith, "John," *Harper's Bible Commentary*, edited by James L. Mays (New York: Harper San Francisco, 1988), 1052.

95 O. V. Jathanna, "Channels of Life: Engaging with Life-affirming, Life-negating and Life-renewing Realities," *Masihi Sevak* XXXII/2 (August 2007), 6-7.

96 Margot Kässmann, "Glimpses of the new Ecumenical Movement," *Echoes* 12 (1997): 39, cited by Indukuri John Mohan Razu, *Global Capitalism as Hydra: A*

enunciates that "theology of life is life-sustaining, life-affirming and life-preserving. In a context where the life of majority is threatened, a counter wailing force vis-à-vis theology that enhances the life of all is apt. What we are experiencing today is nothing but indiscriminate exploitation of the nature and human resources for the benefit of a tiny percentage of people who live across the world."[97] Therefore, as water is a gift of God so also life, God is the source and owner of both water and life. It is this life-giving water affirms life and make the life lived. When the disorders and exploitations like, privatization are removed the life in its fullness is affirmed. This water will satisfy the thirsts for life such as human rights and dignity, liberation in the struggle for justice, peace and integration with the whole creation.

In its declaration on "Water as Life: Water as Right," the UELCI National Theological Colloquium, held in 2004 at Ooty, has affirmed that, "Water is life and denial of water is denial of life."[98] However, both the theological affirmations of water and life cannot be separated from each other rather they are intrinsically intertwined. Thus, the theology of water is that water gives life and water is life.

3.5.4. How to Contravene and Challenge this Evil Power?

According to Vandana Shiva, "Globalization has been presented as purely a trade issue, but it is actually about appropriation of resources. It makes property out of things that have never before been owned as property.... Water, which has always been recognized as a commons, is being privatized. This conflict involves nearly all of humanity and all the species on this planet versus a handful of corporations."[99]

This destructive developmental process has to be countered in order to save the earth and the human community which demands

---

New Look at Market, Money and MNCs (Delhi: ISPCK and Bombay: BUILD, 2006), 270.

97 Indukuri John Mohan Razu, *Global Capitalism as Hydra: A New Look at Market, Money and MNCs* (Delhi: ISPCK and Bombay: BUILD, 2006), 270.

98 "The Ooty Water Declaration," *Waters of Life and Death: Ethical and Theological Responses to Contemporary Water Crises*, edited by Sam P. Mathew & Chandran Paul Martin (Delhi: ISPCK & Chennai: UELCI, 2005), 277.

99 "Quotations About Water" Compiled by Ginger Grab, *The Living Pulpit* (January-March 2005), 48.

strict measures and policies protecting the natural resources and upholding human rights. It can be achieved only when governments take the responsibility and provide legal frameworks for safeguarding the interests of the whole of creation and not just private individuals and corporations. The poor are the hardest hit by this process.[100]

3.5.4.1. Not Commodity but Life-Maker

The process of Privatization does not incorporate the aspirations and needs of people, and it fails to acknowledge the right of water as a right of being a citizen. Instead, it merely reduces to a relationship between service providers and consumers. Maude Barlow and Tony Clarke, while severely critiquing this process, comment:

> *"The commodification of water is wrong – ethically, environmentally and socially. It insures that decisions regarding the allocation of water would centre on commercial, not environmental or social justice consideration. Privatization means that the management of water resources is based on principles of scarcity and profit maximization rather than long-term sustainability. Corporations are dependent on increased consumption to generate profits and are much more likely to invest in the use of chemical technology, destination, marketing and water trading than in conservation."*[101]

Water is a vital and scarce natural resource of the community and the country, and a finite resource. It has to be protected from pollution, contamination depletion, and from private interference and conserved for future generations.[102]

Together with that, we need to uphold the declaration of the Conference on *Water for People and Nature* held in Vancouver in 2001, which says that, "The intrinsic value of the Earth's fresh water precedes its utility and commercial value, and therefore must be respected and safeguarded by all political, commercial, and social institutions; the Earth's fresh water belongs to the Earth and all

100 Anderson H.M. Jeremiah, "Privatization of Water …," 6.

101 *Ibid.*

102 Ramaswamy R. Iyer, *Towards Water Wisdom,* 141.

species, and therefore must not be treated as a private commodity to be bought, sold, and traded for profit; the global fresh water supply is shared legacy, a public trust, and a fundamental human right, and therefore, a collective responsibility."[103] Therefore, we should treat water not as a possession, a commodity, a source of economic advantage for some at the expense of others, but a gift, an outpouring of divine love that reflects Christ's thirst for the wellbeing and full flourishing of the whole creation of which we, with our fragile humanity, are an intimate part.

3.5.4.2. Anthropocentrism to Life-Centeredness: An Alternative Paradigm

Theology, in the twenty-first century, makes a shift from anthropocentrism to *life-centeredness*. That is, the center of theological articulation is not human but life of the whole creation. Konrad Raiser, while discussing about *The World in the Twenty-first Century as Challenges to the Church*, says, "During the past century human community has been separated from its natural setting. Nature became a resource to be used and exploited for the benefit of the human community."[104] The underpinnings behind anthropocentric thoughts have ignored the fact that human life is dependent on nature. Water is one among the other essential factors on which the sustenance of human life depends on.[105] In this sense, *life-centeredness* means that humans have to exercise a caring relationship to *all* living beings and to *all* life-sustaining processes.[106] It is clear that this shift in theology demands to avoid the destructive nature of human activity and to make the interdependence meaningful. Also when hegemonic human powers such as privatization rule over, it presumably becomes self-destructive and purely exclusive. Therefore, this notion of life-centeredness rejects privatization of water and extends to be more inclusive, that is, it includes *life of all creation*.

---

103 Timothy Gorringe, *Harvest: Food, Farming and the Churches*, 89.

104 Konrad Raiser, "The World in the Twenty-first Century: Challenges to the Church," *The Future of Theology: Essays in Honor of Jurgen Moltmann*, 4.

105 *Ibid*., 4-5.

106 *Ibid*., 5.

Here, when nature and its resources are viewed as God's creation, its resources become the gift of God. This implies that water is a gift of/from God and it is given for life sustenance of all creation. Here, theology takes its role to affirm that when water is a gift then no one can claim it authority. No one has the right to privatize or to exploit or to have control over it. When it is privatized then it becomes the violation of the basic fundamental right and in turn, wealth is accumulated on the one side. Therefore, privatization of water is a sin and theologically it cannot be accepted. It needs to be affirmed that water is a God-given gift, to be shared and utilized in common.

Conclusion

We need to be reminded that privatizing water is equal to privatizing God, the source and the giver of life through water. As Aruna Gnanadason urges, "water must not be treated as a *commercial good* or a commodity of trade. As an essential good, it should not be subject to the rules of profit making. Increasingly becoming a scarce good, it must be used sparingly. Water must be placed under public responsibility to guarantee access for all, including the impoverished sectors of society who do not have the purchasing power. This requires that water to be protected as a public good belonging to humanity and *all* life."[107]

107 Aruna Gnanadason, *Listen to the Women! Listen to the Earth!*, 26.

Chapter 4

Theological Reflections of Water and its Significance in the Indian Context

Introduction

Water plays a central and critical role in all aspects of life – in the national environment, in our economies, in food security, in production, in politics. As we have discussed in the first chapter, water has, indeed, a special significance for the great religions. Water has a central place in the practices and beliefs of many religions of the world. This significance manifests itself differently in various religions and beliefs. Yet two particular qualities of water underlie its central place in religions: water is a primary building block of life, a creative force; water cleanses by washing away impurities, purifying objects for ritual use as well as making a person clean, externally and spiritually, ready to come into the presence of the focus of worship.

Caught between growing demand for fresh water on one hand and limited and increasingly polluted water supplies on the other, India still faces difficult choices. Population continues to grow rapidly. Yet there is no more water on earth now than before. Rising demands for water for irrigated agriculture, domestic consumption, and industry are forcing stiff competition over the allocation of scarce water resources among both areas and types of use. This chapter will go further to reflect theologically, by considering the previous discussions, primarily the symbolic significance of water in life and will bring it to the Indian context.

4.1. Need for a Theological Reflection

Today nature is increasingly subjected to domination and exploitation by human civilization where water is not an exemption. Identically, in the name of neo-liberalization the water resources are snatched by a group of money-minded people. This is a threat to water; threat to the source of life; and it challenges the life itself.

The responsibility in creation is given to the human beings in order to rescue the creation from all disasters. The given task, that is, 'to subdue the earth' is with the intension that the protectors of the earth are the human beings and so, they are supposed to keep the creation good. This will create the integrity in creation whereby *Shalom* would prevail. Therefore, theology pays its attention to the economic system of the society. By responding to it practically we have to find a way to protect water and to ensure that everybody can have access to it in an equitable way, not forgetting the other creatures. However, in this theological reflection water primarily stands as a symbol, which signifies and adds it meaning to the reality of our life.

4.2. Water as a Sign and Symbol

Paul Ricoeur, a French Protestant philosopher of the 20th century, in his theories of symbols, asserts that 'symbols give rise to thought.' Therefore, as Ross puts it, it is the task of theology to identify and interpret appropriate symbols through exploring the correlations between life and meaning, which are constantly influenced by the forces at play in the context.[1] In the theological reflection of water, the primary aspect that adds its significance in reality is water being

1 M. M. Ross, "Water for Life, Water of Life and Water as Life...," 81.

signs and symbols. This symbolic connotation of water can be seen in many biblical indications. As the use of symbol in theology becomes significant to express the meaning of life, here the significance of the religious symbol water needs theological enunciation. Using certain hermeneutical tools would bring out this importance of water into life.

4.2.1. Hermeneutical Approach of Christian Theology

Christian theology is engaged in hermeneutical reflection too because it is concerned with the interpretation of the biblical texts and of other religious texts, such as creeds, liturgies, theological writings and spiritual expressions.[2] The scripture also contains the ultimate mystery which can be expressed in symbols. Therefore, allegorical approach needs to be used in this hermeneutical paradigm to expose the mystery hidden in the text (symbol). [3] Here, we use allegorical approach, which provides the input, to water reveal the hidden meaning (mystery) in the symbol of water. Thus, this would contribute to a life-centered theological paradigm and a pertinent atmosphere for the sustainability of all living creatures.

4.2.2. Water as a Symbol of Life

Being conscious of water as a religious symbol Paul Tillich affirms that, "a special character or quality, a power of its own, is attributed to water. By virtue of this natural power, water is situated to become the bearer of a sacred power and thus also become a sacramental element."[4] Furthermore, water is a necessary, an "irreplaceable" religious symbol.[5] It actually participates in the power of that which it symbolizes.

---

2 Werner G. Jeanrond, *Theological Hermeneutics: Developments and Significance* (New York: Crossroad Publishing Company, 1991), 4.

3 *Ibid.*, 21. In the allegorical interpretation the text is understood symbolically: it points beyond itself to a deeper reality (*Ibid.*, 17).

4 Paul Tillich, *The Protestant Era* (Chicago, Illinois: The University of Chicago Press, 1948), 96, quoted by F. W. Dillistone, "The Function of Symbols in Religious Experience," in *Myth and Symbol,* edited by F. W. Dillistone (London: S.P.C.K., 1966), 7.

5 F. W. Dillistone, "The Function of Symbols in Religious Experience," 7.

Leonardo Da Vinci said, "Water is the driver of life."[6] In the biblical-theological use it is clear that water constitutes the life of Israelites. Their daily life and bread depended upon water. In fact, water is allied with the life of non-human beings. Even in the fertility of trees and plant life, in its entirety, is directly linked with the presence of abundant water (Ps.1: 3; Ezk.17: 5, 8; etc.). At the mere scent of water a tree will bud, even after it has been cut down (Job.14:19).[7]

4.2.2.1. Water for Life

The declaration of the United Nations as the decade 2005-2015 as the international decade for "Water for Life" has gained the universal significance for this theological expression. This recognizes that water is needed for life sustenance with its call for safe clean water, a secure and close supply and improved sanitation for the world's population. This can be perceived in relation to our lives. When Ross relates the need of water for the origination of life, he writes: "The theory that most life originated in the salty ocean waters does make sense from the facts of one-half of our bodies being constituted by water and of the presence of salt in our blood. Further, mammals, including humans, are born from embryonic fluid, which is water."[8] Moreover, it is fresh water that gives life to all. In fact, 60% of the population is dehydrated. This is not because people are not drinking enough fluid; it is because they are not drinking enough of the right fluid, water. At just 2% dehydration a person's performance decreases by around 20%. A human body is 70% water. A human brain has 15 billion brain cells, these are between 74% and 85% water. Therefore,

---

6 Quoted by S. V. S. Rana, *Essentials of Ecology and Environmental Science* (New Delhi: Prentice-Hall of India, 2003), 224, cited by Sebastian Kochupurackal, *Eco-Mission: A Paradigm Shift in Missiology* (Bangalore: Asian Trading Corporation, 2007), 95.

7 D. T. Tsumara, "Water," *New Dictionary of Biblical Theology*, edited by Desmond Alexander and Brian S. Rosner (Leicester, England: Inter-Varsity Press, 2000), 840.

8 M. M. Ross, "Water for Life, Water of Life and Water as Life..," 83.

to get the best performance out of one's body a person has to put the best in, fresh water, with nothing added.[9]

However, the life slogan 'water for life' makes a critical point that water is primarily meant for supporting life. Thus, for the human survival water is very much needed and everyone needs water to live. Here, the minimal ethical sense in relation to life and water demands that we adopt life-styles that will make water available for us and at the same time we need to preserve water resource for future generations as well. In this way, the role of water and its qualities call us to the redemptive life both theologically and symbolically.[10]

4.2.2.2. Water of Life

This reflection is mostly of the relation of water with the aspects of life. 'Life' is a reality that has so many dimensions to it that has to be discussed from various angles. 'Water' serves as a symbol of life itself and at the same time, points to God who is the foundation of all, that is, of life, water and of the human.[11] By the virtue of its numerous uses it becomes a symbol or a paradigm. In the religious realm water is much associated with Christian tradition. Water can be a threat to creation (destructive waters). At the same time, in Baptism, water becomes a symbol of our reconstitution in divine action. Here, it is used in twofold meanings: water as that which drowns (and in the process totally removes sin) and water as that refreshes.[12] Water is a paradigm of life. This could be traced from the biblical sources. As the Bible describes Eden as garden we can see a river having four tributaries. These four gave life to all living creatures with their waters. The Jeremianic traditions see God as the source of life in the metaphor of water (Jer.2:13). Perhaps Jesus would have drawn these traditions for his symbolical speech when he said that He as the fountain of living water and whoever drinks of him does not thirst of water again. Furthermore, Revelation views a restored community where the 'river of the water of life' was flowing from

9 "Water for life," *Challenge Newsline*, Issue 60 (April 2006), 4.

10 M. M. Ross, "Water for Life, Water of Life and Water as Life..," 84.

11 *Ibid.*, 85.

12 See *Ibid.*, 86-89.

the throne of God and of the lamb.[13] Here, we have to embrace the implied meaning that water is fused with 'life' alone. However, these reflections remind us that water serves as the symbolism of 'life'.

These discussions lead us to realize the propinquity between water and life, between symbol and the signified reality. Every symbol should lead to reality whereby the inter-connectedness of life and meaning is obtained. In such direction, water takes us to reality of life and all that has to do with life. Therefore, we need to realize that water is a gift from God and to treat it as anything else is to act in opposition to God. Thus, it is clear that "privatization of drinking water is a cruel and unjust approach, which questions even the survival of the living creatures."[14]

4.3. Indian milieu

The so-called "victory of capitalism" in the 1990s has opened the floodgates for the increased influence of the capitalist market economy around the globe.[15] India became one of the targets of neo-liberal hegemony through which India's water and related resources are being privatized. The people of India face many consequences due to this privatization (some consequences are already mentioned in the second chapter). When the land-based resources are becoming limited and more degraded, unequivocally it affects the lives of people. If this is the situation of the people living in non-desert area, it is unimaginable to assess the condition when the water table gets lower in desert communities, which is still posing a threat to the existence of the poor and water security. Now, as Archana Sinha expresses, "India's statistics show an alarming trend that rapid population growth will lead to greater demand for an increasingly smaller supply of water resources. Nowhere else in the world does population growth

---

13 John Samuel, "Towards a Biblical Understanding of Water," *Waters of Life and Death: Ethical and Theological Responses to Contemporary Water Crises*, edited by Sam Peedikayil Mathew & Chandran Paul Martin (Delhi: ISPCK & Chennai: UELCI, 2005), 208.

14 Sebastian Kochupurackal, *Eco-Mission: A Paradigm Shift in Missiology* (Bangalore: Asian Trading Corporation, 2007), 98.

15 Joerg Riege, "The Economy Is Expanding: Theology to the Rescue?," *Religious Studies Review* 28/3 (July 2002), 215.

and poverty play such a large role in affecting water resource issues. Poverty and reduced access to safe water resources has limited the ability of the poor to improve their situation, which has only served to perpetuate the poverty cycle especially among rural population and women."[16] This is the Indian reality in terms of water stress.

4.4. Groaning for Liberation

In a country like India, groaning for liberation is two-folded. The people of the land groan for liberation from the clutches of privatization is on the one side and groaning of water for its liberation from privatizing it is on the other.

Just like the Israelites were taken as captives to Egypt, suffered under the economy of Pharaoh and cried out for liberation from the bondage of Egypt, today the Indian people and the water resources are groaning for their liberation from the bondage of neo-liberal economy of multinationals, which privatize water and related resources in India. In the Bible, we see that after God liberated Israelites from Egypt, "God's homeless or landless people's journey to the promised land is very important. God made them a landed people."[17] This promised land is blessed with flowing streams, springs, ground water and rain (Deut.8:7; 11:11). A land with enough water sources is very important in their life, because they were landless and most of them were struggling for water in the wilderness. One person's right on his/her father's land includes water sources. Achsah, daughter of Caleb claimed for a land with springs of water from her father (Jos.15:19). The Samaritan woman (in the NT) clearly communicates this message to Jesus that they got a well from their

16 Archana Sinha, *Gender Dynamics in Water Security: A Study in Rajasthan* (New Delhi: Indian Social Institute, 2005), 2-3.

17 Walter Bruegemann, *The Land,* (4th Reprint, 1986) (Philadelphia: Fortress Press, 1946), 1-15, cited by K.J. Philip, "A Theological and Ethical Response to Water Crisis in the Tribal Areas in Plachimada," *Waters of Life and Death: Ethical and Theological Responses to Contemporary Water Crises*, edited by Sam Peedikayil Mathew & Chandran Paul Martin (Delhi: ISPCK & Chennai: UELCI, 2005), 82.

ancestor Jacob (Jn.4:12).[18] 'Every person needs to have enough water' is the biblical ethics. Here in the Indian context, the multinationals permeated into our land, pilfered the water resources and ruling the citizens of the land with their neo-liberal capitalism. Now, these evil forces have to be rooted out of the country and the people of the land have to regain their water resources for their livelihood. Water and related resources, being the gift of God, have to be liberated from the clutches of these evil powers.

4.5. What Can be Done?

When the livelihood of the Indian people is worsened day by day due to privatization of water, and when people groan for liberation along with the water resources to have a better life situation is not in the near future. Rather the process towards better future could be handled with the following proposed models:

4.5.1. Towards an Alternate Economy

The historical and biblical overview demonstrates that there is a basic decision before us: Shall the economy serve the accumulation of property for a few owners or shall it serve the life of all people and the earth? Neo-liberal globalization shows that an economic system following the deregulated rules of the market based on the absolute right of private property and unlimited accumulation through money mechanisms leads to destruction and even self-destruction. It is not possible to repair the damage produced by this system. All efforts by governments or by the UN since the 1980s to stop the destructive effects of the global system framed by neo-liberalism have been in vain. Public debt is growing everywhere, social exclusion and degradation as well as the destruction of nature are increasing around the globe. So, we need to reconstruct the basic foundations of our economy. A key element in this is private property because the whole credit, production and distribution system is built on private property. It operates according to the principle: "to all those who

18 K. J. Philip, "A Theological and Ethical Response to Water Crisis in the Tribal Areas in Plachimada," *Waters of Life and Death: Ethical and Theological Responses to Contemporary Water Crises*, edited by Sam Peedikayil Mathew & Chandran Paul Martin (Delhi: ISPCK & Chennai: UELCI, 2005), 82-83.

have, more will be given; but from those who have nothing, even what they have will be taken away".[19]

Therefore, an alternate economy is very much demanded above all these mutilating economic structures. As we have seen above, biblical-based economy, which gives importance to people and sustainability of all resources, would be an appropriate economy here. God the Creator is the Economist who provides the household to the creation for their livelihood. The description of M. Douglas Meeks, who proposes the metaphor *God the Economist,* would be meaningful here. He states that "Economy[20] means literally *the law or the management of the household.*"[21] For him, household is the household of God; it is not the modern notion of family consuming unit but "it is connected with the production, distribution, and consumption of the necessities of life. It is the site of economy, the site of human livelihood."[22] Meeks further describes what should be the most survival principle for an alternate economic system. He writes: "Every person has economic and political rights. The land and all of its fruition is a gift of God which is meant to be used as the means of God's righteousness, as a means toward the fullness of the life of all of God's children and of the whole creation. To be human means to have a right to life-giving share of the world's resources so that one can serve God's life-giving economy for the creation."[23] D. Dhanaraj, in his discussion on integrity of creation, conveys this as one of the intentions of God in the work creation – that is, "to design the natural world to be the *OIKOS* for all the diverse eco-systems including the humans to live and find sustenance in it, closely knit together on the principle of peaceful and harmonious co-existence."[24]

---

19 Ulrich Duchrow, "Private Property: A Growing Danger for life…," 477.

20 The Greek word from which we derive economy, *oikonomia*, is a compound of *oikos*, which means "household" and *nomos*, which means "law" or "management".

21 M. Douglas Meeks, *God the Economist: The Doctrine of God and Political Economy* (Minneapolis: Fortress Press, 1989), 3.

22 *Ibid.*

23 *Ibid.*, 91.

24 D. Dhanaraj, "Integrity of Creation – A Theological Perspective," *The Sathri Journal* 1/1 (January 2006), 93.

However, thus, this economy gives life to all creation and the well being of not only human but the whole creation is integrated in this economy.

4.5.2. Community Ownership of Water

Land, natural resources and the environment are goods which should not be owned in the sense of *dominium*, of absolute private ownership; there should be only the right of usage.[25] The same conversion towards life and the common good is necessary with the ownership form of basic social services. It has already become clear how disastrous the consequences are for the majority of people, particularly in pauperized countries, when water supplies are privatized, i.e., transferred to the ownership form of the capitalist market of profit maximization.[26]

In the dialogue between the Samaritan woman and Jesus, the Samaritan woman makes a reference that the well she was drawing water from had belonged to their forefather's and that his sons and flock had drunk from it (Jn. 4:12). In this text, we observe that it does point to ancient sources of water that were community owned and were used to serve the interests of all. In India, also we have such ownership of water resources. The most notable of these of course is tribal water resources.[27] Moreover, it would be appropriate to think that we need to regain the earlier community-based water management systems that India had before the British rule. Some of the community based water management initiatives are: a) Rural water harvest, which is the traditional rain water harvesting; b) Tank management, in which small tanks have to be constructed, each covering a small command area, which is more sustainable in the long run; and c) Watershed management, which is defined as a geo-hydrological unit draining to a common point by a system of drains and it is a logical unit for planning the optimal development of its soil,

25 Ulrich Duchrow, "Private Property: A Growing Danger for life…," 478.

26 *Ibid.*, 479.

27 Philip Vinod Peacock, "Water Conflict," 57.

water biomass resources.[28] These initiatives require integrated and participatory approach from each community. Such a community based water owning and management would enhance corporate existence and collective life of all creatures.

4.5.3. A Paradigm Shift from Growth Model[29] to *Shalom* Model

In India, we have been familiarized with this growth model, which exploits the public and the resources under the umbrella of "development." By this model, what has happened is the growth of the western industries at our cost. As we critically look at this model, we also need to address the drinking water issue decisively. By considering the cases of both India and China, Ulrich Duchrow, clearly states that this growth, which has been carried out under the umbrella system of neo-liberalism, is not sustainable and "this growth itself is producing more and more inequality, plus social and particularly ecological problems."[30] Water is also taken under this ideological menace where the western companies increase their growth and look for more profit by using massive capital and exploiting the water resources of our land. At the end, it creates disparities and ecological imbalances. Therefore, we need to take a shift from this growth model to *Shalom* model.

---

28 Vandana Panwar, "Techniques of Water Management and Conservation," *Vikas Vani Journal* II/2 (April-June 2008), 16-17.

29 Growth model is a paradigm of development, the western industrial growth model, which is universally accepted. In this process of growth, capital is used enormously and natural resources, particularly the non-renewable one, are ruthlessly exploited. The goods are produced in this process according to the demand of the consumerist economy where the controlling logic of growth is greed and not need. It creates imbalances between different sectors and allows massive exploitation of the rural and natural environment for the benefit of the dominant classes. This profit oriented growth destroys the eco-balance (K.C. Abraham, *Liberative Solidarity: Contemporary Perspectives on Mission* [Thiruvalla: Christava Sahitya Samithi, 1996], 113).

30 Ulrich Duchrow, "Difficulties and Opportunities for Theology in Today's World," *Another Possible World: Reclaiming Liberation Theology*, edited by Marcella Maria Althaus-Reid, Ivan Petrella and Luiz Carlos Susin (London: SCM Press, 2007), 18-19.

"Shalom" is, of course, the Hebrew word most often translated as "peace". Its basic meaning is wholeness; a state of harmony among God, humanity and all of creation. Walter Bruegemann, a well known Old Testament theologian, wrote thus: "The central vision of world history in the Bible is that all of creation is one, every creature in community with every other, living in harmony and security toward the joy and well-being of every other creature. ... *Shalom* is the substance of the biblical vision of one community embracing all creation." Bruce C. Birch clearly intends this that "a full understanding of *Shalom* begins with creation. *Shalom* is God's intention for creation from the beginning. All elements of creation are interrelated. Each element participates in the whole of creation, and if any element is denied wholeness and well-being (*Shalom*), all are thereby diminished. This relational character of creation is rooted in all creatures' common origin in a God who not only created all that is but who continues to be active in the world, seeking our *Shalom*."[31] The *Shalom* is the wellness, the wholeness intended for all creation. That is, here by the integrity of all creation is expected and from this integrity the *Shalom* exists. When this model is adopted water gets its due respect and significance from human beings and is shared to all creations irrespective of their divisions.

4.6. How Best Can We Respond to Water Issue?

We have discussed previously that the quality of water is constantly decreasing by the use of artificially produced chemical fertilizers, detergents and industrial and communal wastes which get into the water cycle and often contain poisonous substances. So, the water which has been meant by God as our resource of life is changing into the water bringing death. The problem is directly connected with the water treatment and water sanitation. Only a small proportion of the human population is privileged to have water sanitation and clean water at a sufficient level. Another serious threat to the water cycle is caused by the global warming and by the fact that more and more water evaporates into the atmosphere – this further contributes

31 Bruce C. Birch, "Old Testament Foundations for Peacemaking in the Nuclear Era," *The Christian Century*, (December 4, 1985): 1115.

to global warming and has disastrous effects on many regions of the world.

It is a vital situation that we need to respond to this issue of water crisis and privatization. We need to be more practical in order to conserve water as far as we can. First of all, we have to reject and ignore privatization of water and we ought to take few measures to save water for our use. The following suggestions could be considered in response to water crisis:

- We need to get better at catching the rain where it falls and before it disperses.
- There needs to be a considerable revolution in the way we use water. Most homes can make big savings.
- And more than that urban waste water should be recycled to make clean drinking water.
- The simple truth is that, to protect our rivers and ensure water supplies in the future, we have to use less water. We have to change our perception of seeing water as a free resource, available in unlimited quantities as of right.
- To be more and more practical we all have to join in to save water as best we can, turning off taps, fixing leaks, watering plants at night, having shorter showers, sparing the toilet flush sometimes. New houses should be built water smart, plumbed to catch rainwater and recycle washing water to flush toilets and water gardens.

4.6.1. Church's Response

There are different problems pertaining to lack of drinking water in our country. Church, being part of the society, in no way can escape from the realities of the society. Church has to respond to the economic life of the people. Particularly, church has to show its practical response to privatization of water. Church has to recognize its responsibilities of environmental stewardship and economic justice through biblical studies and a theology of water.

Duchrow's suggestion could be considered in our churches to put an end to these evil forces. He writes thus:

> *"Prophetic critique and resistance is needed regarding the global market, implemented by neo-liberal power, which totalizes the mechanism of capital accumulation based on private property, idolizes itself and is increasingly destroying the life of people and the earth. The churches, on the basis of their biblical traditions, have a unique mandate and responsibility to reintroduce this issue into the debate on globalization. Living alternatives are needed regarding the use of church property, money and land, which must be used exclusively under social, ecological and democratic criteria. Intervention for legal political reforms is needed regarding many demands asked for by the victims of neo-liberal globalization."*[32]

One of the problems we find in the society is that of lack of drinking water for people and opportunities for people depending on water (fishers, farmers). What we can do is that we can introduce the best water-saving practices in our parishes, church centers and inform the public about it. By this we can set up an example for our communities. We can also support or develop campaigns informing about water issues in our area and about best possible practices related to water. Another problem is regarding increasing environmental, economic and social costs connected with water distribution and delivery, water treatment and sanitation. We should try to develop and to support local and regional solutions for water systems into which clean drinking water would be taken with minimum treatment and by shortest possible distribution way from local resources. At the same time, the used water should be returned purified by us as users. Ideally this should apply for all sorts of church buildings and institutions. At the same time, we need to adopt all possible practices in order to minimize pollution, reduced consumption and necessary water protection and water savings should be implemented and promoted.

At present, church seems to be silent in conserving natural resources such as water. Being silent, tend to mean that church is indirectly going in par with the neo-economic and neo-liberal ideologies. Though, church may seem to actively participate in the

32 Ulrich Duchrow, "Private Property: A Growing Danger for life…," 480.

liberation of people it lacks its action in working for the liberation of the natural resources. Ecological awareness in a larger level and awareness about water, which constitutes life, in particular, has to be created among the people. Even preachings in the pulpit should include this and should call for the resistance of the social evil called privatization. To be concerned with the life of its people does not mean that it has nothing to do with nature and related resources, so as to with water. Moreover, as life is intrinsically intertwined with water, Church needs to have a new vision of life-centeredness. It is the challenge before the church to move from anthropocentrism to life-centered spirituality and ethics.

However, it may seem difficult to do or implement all these steps but everybody can do at least something for water. The implementation of some procedures suggested above would require sound technical or environmental knowledge and resources. Other practical steps require only good will and more attention towards the God's gifts, of which one is also the water which we touch.

Conclusion

Beginning with the 1970s, we have seen the emergence of neo-liberalism. The forces of capital operate more and more on a global level, putting pressure on the national political and legal instruments which had been able to make property socially responsible. This has very destructive consequences. But nature also suffers destruction owing to an economic system operating towards one end: maximization of profit on capital property.[33] As populations grow and water use per person rises, demand for freshwater is increasing. Yet the supply of freshwater is finite and threatened by pollution and the forces of privatization. The privatization of water has particularly deadly consequences. In the poorer countries, as we have seen, privatization process is transforming water into a means of accumulating capital property by excluding the poor from the most fundamental human right and quenching of their thirst by drinking water.[34]

33 Ulrich Duchrow, "Private Property: A Growing Danger for life…," 474.

34 *Ibid.*, 481.

Therefore, there is a need to acknowledge the seriousness of water scarcity and access to clean drinking water that we are facing. As we discussed above, we have to recognize the significance of water in our life and in the life of all creation. Water signifies largely in every realm of our life. Every individual needs to have an inner awareness and should have precautionary mechanism in every day life, considering the neighborhood of all creation. If we fail to use the water resources in a sustainable way and if we fail to initiate programmes of conservation of water it will intensify in future. As many water experts say even by the year 2025 India may have to face serious water crisis. To avoid these crises, we must conserve water, pollute less, and manage supply and demand.

Conclusion

Water is a precious, life-giving and pure resource of the earth, which God gifted to all creation. Water is visible, a living symbol of cleanliness, cool refreshment, fertility. Water symbolizes the primal substances from which all forms come and to which they will return. It is the principle of what is formless and potential, basis of every cosmic manifestation and container of all seeds. As Loren Wilkinson sees, "like the air, water circulates freely and binds us in a community of living things."[1]

As a preexisted element before creation of the world, water has a great regard in the religions. A common thread to all the religions that we have already discussed such as, in Hinduism, Islam, Buddhism, Sikhism, Zoroastrianism, Judaism, and Christianity, is the sacred quality of water in which water has a major role to play in the act of purification. In purification, it signifies the inner purity and cleanliness of the believers. Water is regarded as sacred for it gives a real meaning to the one who uses it. The use of water with a sacred intention brings together reintegration and creation. In any religion, when water is used in a ritual it becomes holy after it is blessed, as in the Baptism of Christianity. Moreover, water has been given a divine status in religions, like, Hinduism and Zoroastrianism. We see that in Zoroastrianism water is equated with that of a deity, *Varuna* and

1 Loren Wilkinson, *Earth Keeping in the Nineties: Stewardship of Creation* (Grand Rapids, Michigan: William B. Eerdmans Publishing Company, 1991), 5.

more than that water is being worshipped and sacrifices are being offered to water. However, in religions, water is portrayed as a life-giving force. It is the source of all life. Since it is used for drinking it becomes more significant in the life of all creation. Water is needed everywhere and at every level of existence as the source of life and growth.

The issue of clean and safe drinking water became one of the most critical natural resource issues that humanity faces. As of now the supply of freshwater available to humanity is shrinking because many freshwater resources have become increasingly polluted. Rivers and other water resources have become receptacles for a degraded collection of wastes from municipal sewage, toxic industrial effluents, and harmful chemicals. Also, use of pesticides and other chemicals in agricultural activities pollute ground waters. Climate crisis results in floods, floods, cyclones, heat waves, and droughts. Communities in water-stressed countries are beginning to compete with one another for prior use of this precious resource, which finally ends in conflicts within the nation. The scarcity of water shows awful effects in the liaison of water with women, children, Dalits and Tribals. "Safe drinking water is a fundamental right" is denied for common people in India in its process of economic globalization. The natural rights such as water rights are buried due to the intrusion of neo-liberal ideology like, privatization. The National Water Policies do not seem to help the common people of India. The state and central governments have to be forced to take precautionary measures to reduce, avoid, and get rid of these issues related to water and let every one to use water in a sensible way.

Privatization of water, in India, is getting rooted deeply as the European companies plant their projects with the neoliberal ideological claims. The Indian situation on privatization of water is becoming a national problem. It creates serious consequences such as economic disparity, ecological imbalance and usurps the public control of water. In fact, caricaturing of privatization leads people towards darkness and hopelessness. With its pseudo neo-liberal creeds it also created a culture of bottled water for which water resources are unjustly exploited. Therefore, it is the need of the hour that we have to resist these evil forces.

Theological critique is one possible mode to resist privatization of water. Various theological reflections affirm the significance of water in relation to life. When we talk about creation in theological terms within the perspectives of eco-theology, the stewardship of human beings is always proposed against their domination. This has to be considered in terms of water as well. Safeguarding the earth and its resources is a mandate given by God to human beings. With the same perspective we have to take biblical-theology as a primary tool for making a theological critique for privatization of water. Water is the basis of life of all creation. It is an inherited resource from God for God gifted it freely to all creation and thus God is the owner of water. Therefore, water should not be misappropriated by vested interests and should not be subjected to the any form of domination and exploitation. Thus, privatizing water and related resources is usurping God's ownership on water. To defy this, we need to see privatization of water as 'Leviathan' for it is crooked and with its twisting nature, creates chaos in the regularity. Privatization of water is tyrant in nature because it oppresses the poor, including women and children, with its autocratic domination. With its leviathanic nature privatization changes the whole economy of the country and misleads people into the state of darkness.

However, hitherto, we saw water serves as an important element for life itself. Therefore, the notion "water of life" significantly substantiates the critique of privatization. Water contains life in itself which becomes a life force to human and nonhuman beings. Even with its symbolic nature water brings the reality that signifies to life. Therefore, a theology of water should be a theology of life for without water there is no life.

Thus, it is apparent that human beings are not given a power either to misuse it or to have power over it. Rather it should be understood that since water is a life-centered factor there is a need to create a pertinent atmosphere for the sustainability of all living creatures. For this, we have to change our perspective from anthropocentrism to life-centeredness which would help us to acknowledge the life of all. We have to release the captives, both water and the people of India, from the clutches of neo-liberal economy of multinationals, which privatize water and related resources in India.

Therefore, an alternate economy is very much required above all these mutilating economic structures. Biblical-based economy, which gives importance to people and sustainability of all resources, is recommended here. We see God the Creator is the Economist who provides the household to the creation for their livelihood. I have also proposed that we should to take a shift from *growth model*, which exploits the public and the natural resources under the umbrella of "development" to *Shalom* model, where by the wellbeing and wholeness of all creation are intended and in which the integrity of all creation is visualized.

Water, as a vital element to life, should not be subjected to the rules of profit making. Since it is becoming a scarce resource we must use it cautiously. Water must be placed under public responsibility to ensure equal access to all. Water, a vast part of God's created world, is an inherent gift to be shared; to be valued; and to be protected. Church, as the community of faith, being part of the society, has a crucial role in the realities of the society. On the basis of biblical traditions, church has a mandate and responsibility to initiate the issue of privatization into the discussion on globalization. It has to respond to the economic life of the people. Church has to respond practically to privatization of water. Being silent with regard to ecological jeopardy, particularly, with privatization of water, would mean that church goes in par with the neo-liberal ideologies. To work for water is to work for peoples' life. Therefore, church must include the goal "struggling for precious water is struggling for life" in its mission.

Bibliography

Books

Abraham, K. C. *Liberative Solidarity: Contemporary Perspectives on Mission.* Thiruvalla: Christava Sahitya Samithi, 1996.

____________. *Transforming Vision: Theological – Methodological Paradigm Shifts.* Tiruvalla: Christava Sahitya Samithi.

Agarwal, K. C. *Environmental Biology.* Bikaner, India: Agro Botanical Publishers, 1993.

Al Gore, Senator. *Earth in the Balance: Ecology and the Human Spirit.* London: Houghton Mifflin Company, 1992.

Aleaz, K. P. "Waters in Vedic-Post Vedic Traditions." In *Water Struggle.* Edited by V. J. John. Kolkata: Bishop's College & Delhi: ISPCK, 2007.

Annan, Kofi. "Forward." In *Water for People: Water for Life. (United Nations World Water Development Report).* New York: UNESCO & Berghahn Books, 2003.

Arul, Carolin. *Water Laws and Rights in India.* Delhi: ISPCK & Chennai: UELCI, 2005.

Baartmans, Frans. *APAH, The Sacred Waters: An Analysis of a Primordial Symbol in Hindu Myths.* Delhi: B.R. Publishing Corporation, 1990.

Barbour, Ian G. *Religion and Science: Historical and Contemporary Issues.* New York: Harper Collins Publishers, 1997.

Barlow, Maude and Tony Clarke. *Blue Gold: The Fight to Stop the Corporate Theft of the World's Water.* New Delhi: Left Word Books, 2003.

Boyce, Mary. *A History of Zoroastrianism.* Vol. I. Netherlands: E. J. Brill and Leiden, 1975.

Buch, Maganlal A. *Zoroastrian Ethics.* Baroda: A. G. Widegery, 1919.

Chakravarthi, Jayati. "Water in Religions." In *Humane Response to Water Crisis.* Edited by D. John Chelladurai. Nagpur: India Peace Centre, 2006.

D'Cruz, Wendell. *A Warli-Christian Story: An Experiment in Story Theology.* New Delhi: ISPCK, 1999.

Derr, Thomas Sieger. *Ecology and Human Liberation: A Theological Critique of the Use and Abuse of Our Birthright.* Geneva: World Council of Churches, 1973.

Dillistone, F. W. "The Function of Symbols in Religious Experience." In *Myth and Symbol.* Edited by F.W. Dillistone. London: S.P.C.K., 1966.

Dogra, Bharat. "Water Crisis Manmade." In *Environment Protection Challenges and Issues: Impact of Rapid Development and Policy Measures.* Edited by V. S. Mahajan. New Delhi: Deep & Deep Publications, 1993.

Duchrow, Ulrich. "Difficulties and Opportunities for Theology in Today's World." In *Another Possible World: Reclaiming Liberation Theology.* Edited by Marcella Maria Althaus-Reid, Ivan Petrella and Luiz Carlos Susin. London: SCM Press, 2007.

Dwivedi and B. N. Tiwari. *Environmental Crisis and Hindu Religion.* New Delhi: Gitanjali Publishing House, 1987.

Eliade, Mircea. *Patterns in Comparative Religion.* London: Sheed and Ward, 1971.

Gelderloos, Orin G. *Eco-Theology: The Judeo-Christian Tradition and the Politics of Ecological Decision Making.* Glasgow: Wild Goose Publications, 1992.

Gnanadason, Aruna. *Listen to the Women! Listen to the Earth!* Geneva: WCC Publications, 2005.

Gorringe, Timothy. *Harvest: Food, Farming and the Churches.* London: SPCK, 2006.

Hardtke, Astrid. "Privatizing God's Treasure for the World." In *Water: God's Gift for Life.* Edited by Judi Fisher. Geneva, Switzerland: World Alliance of Reformed Churches, 2006.

Iyer, Ramaswamy R. *Water: Perspectives, Issues, Concerns.* New Delhi: Sage Publications, 2003.

_______________. *Towards Water Wisdom: Limits, Justice, Harmony.* New Delhi: Sage Publications, 2007.

Jacob, Louis. *The Jewish Religion: A Companion.* Oxford, New York: Oxford University Press, 1995.

Jeanrond, Werner G. *Theological Hermeneutics: Developments and Significance.* New York: Crossroad Publishing Company, 1991.

Jones, Bevan. *The People of the Mosque.* (Fifth edition). Delhi: ISPCK and Madras: CLS, 1980.

Kirkpatrick, Clifton. "Introduction to the Theme." In *Water: God's Gift for Life.* Edited by Judi Fisher. Geneva, Switzerland: World Alliance of Reformed Churches, 2006.

Kochupurackal, Sebastian. *Eco-Mission: A Paradigm Shift in Missiology.* Bangalore: Asian Trading Corporation, 2007.

Korten, David C. *When Corporations Rule the World.* USA: Kumarian Press and Barrett-Koehler Publishers, 1995.

Larsson, Per. *"Your will be done on earth…" – Ecological Theology for Asia: An Ecumenical Textbook for Theological Schools.* Hong Kong, China: Christian Conference of Asia, 2004.

Lazareth, William H. and Nikos Nissiotis. *Baptism, Eucharist and Ministry.* (Faith and Order Paper no.111). Geneva: World Council of Churches, 1982.

Meeks, M. Douglas. *God the Economist: The Doctrine of God and Political Economy.* Minneapolis: Fortress Press, 1989.

Millar, Roland E. *Muslim Friends: Their Faith and Feeling – An Introduction to Islam.* Chennai, India: Orient Longman, 2000.

Modi, Jivanji Jamshedji. *The Naojote Ceremony of the Parsees.* (Second edition). Bombay: Fort Printing Press, 1914.

Moltmann, Jurgen. *God in Creation: An Ecological Doctrine of Creation.* London: SCM Press Ltd., 1985.

________________. *The Source of Life: The Holy Spirit and the Theology of Life.* London: SCM Press, 1997.

Morrish, Ivor. *The Thoughtful Guide to Religion.* New Delhi: Pentagon Press, 2007.

Nair, Rashmi. "Modern Colonialism." In *Water [sold] is Life, Right.* (A pamphlet). Bangalore: SCMI, n.d.

Nalunnakkal, George Mathew. *Green Liberation: Towards an Integral Ecotheology.* Delhi: ISPCK/NCCI, 1999.

Pangborn, Cyrus R. *Zoroastrianism: A Beleaguered Faith.* New Delhi: Vikas Publishing House, 1982.

Panikkar, Raimundo. *The Vedic Experience Mantramanjari: An Anthology of the Vedas for Modern Man and Contemporary Celebration.* London: Darton, Longman & Todd, 1977.

Peacock, Philip Vinod. "Water Conflict." In *Waters of Life and Death: Ethical and Theological Responses to Contemporary Water Crises.* Edited by Sam Peedikayil Mathew & Chandran Paul Martin. Delhi: ISPCK & Chennai: UELCI, 2005.

Peruma, Joseph. *The Motherly Earth: An Ecological Ethics of Human-Nature Relationship*. Bangalore: Claretian Publications, 2002.

Philip, K. J. "A Theological and Ethical Response to Water Crisis in the Tribal Areas in Plachimada." In *Waters of Life and Death: Ethical and Theological Responses to Contemporary Water Crises*. Edited by Sam Peedikayil Mathew & Chandran Paul Martin. Delhi: ISPCK & Chennai: UELCI, 2005.

Raiser, Konrad. "The World in the Twenty-first Century: Challenges to the Church." In *The Future of Theology: Essays in Honor of Jurgen Moltmann.* Edited by Miroslav Volf, Carmen Krieg and Thomas Kucharz. Grand Rapids, Michigan: William B. Eerdmans Publishing Company, 1996.

Rajkumar, Christopher. "Inclusive Need for Interlinking of Rivers." In *Inclusive Growth in Globalised India: Challenges and Options*. Edited by Jagadish Gandhi. New Delhi: Deep & Deep Publications, 2008.

Ramanathan, Usha. *Legislating for Water: The Indian Context.* (IELRC Working Paper 1992-1). Geneva: International Environmental Law Research Centre, 1992.

Rao, Seshagiri. "The Five Great Elements (*Pancamahabhuta*): An Ecological Perspective." In *Hinduism and Ecology: The Intersection of Earth, Sky and Water*. Edited by Christopher Key Chapple and Mary Evelyn Tucker. NewDelhi: Oxford University Press, 2000.

Razu, Indukuri John Mohan. *Global Capitalism as Hydra: A New Look at Market, Money and MNCs.* Delhi: ISPCK and Bombay: BUILD, 2006.

Razu, John Mohan. "Water for People, Water for Life: An Ethical (Christian) Response." In *Waters of Life and Death: Ethical and Theological Responses to Contemporary Water Crises*. Edited by Sam Peedikayil Mathew & Chandran Paul Martin. Delhi: ISPCK & Chennai: UELCI, 2005.

Ross, M. M. "Water for Life, Water of Life and Water as Life: Meaning and Symbol in Theology." In *Water Struggle*. Edited by V. J. John. Kolkata: Bishop's College & Delhi: ISPCK, 2007.

Samuel, John. "Towards a Biblical Understanding of Water." In *Waters of Life and Death: Ethical and Theological Responses to Contemporary Water Crises*. Edited by Sam Peedikayil Mathew & Chandran Paul Martin. Delhi: ISPCK & Chennai: UELCI, 2005.

Sangeetha, D. Rebecca. "Genderization of Water." In *Waters of Life and Death: Ethical and Theological Responses to Contemporary Water Crises*. Edited by Sam Peedikayil Mathew & Chandran Paul Martin. Delhi: ISPCK & Chennai: UELCI, 2005.

Sarkar, R. L. *The Bible, Ecology and Environment.* Delhi: ISPCK, 2000.

Schneider, Ann Kathrin and Uwe Hoering. *King Customer? The World Bank's "new" Water Policy and its Implementation in India and Sri Lanka.* Mumbai: Vikas Adhyayan Kendra, 2005.

Shiva, Vandana. *Water Wars: Privatization, Pollution, and Profit.* New Delhi: India Research Press, 2002.

Shiva, Vandana and Kunwar Jalees. *Sujalam: Living Waters. The Impact of the River Linking Project.* New Delhi: NAVDANYA, 2003.

Shiva, Vandana. *Globalization's New wars: Seed, Water and Life Forms.* New Delhi: Women Unlimited, 2005.

Silva, Lily de. "Man and Nature in a Mutual Causal Relationship." In *Man in Nature: Guest or Engineer?* Edited by S. J. Samartha and Lynn de Silva. Colombo: The Ecumenical Institute for Study and Dialogue & Geneva: The World Council of Churches, 1979.

Silva, Lynn de. *Buddhism: Beliefs and Practices in Sri Lanka.* (Second revised edition). Colombo, 1980.

Singh, Arun Kumar. *Privatization of Rivers in India.* Mumbai: Vikas Adhyan Kendra, 2004.

Singh, I. J. *Sikhs and Sikhism: A View with a Bias.* New Delhi: Manohar Publishers, 1994.

Sinha, Archana. *Gender Dynamics in Water Security: A Study in Rajasthan.* New Delhi: Indian Social Institute, 2005.

Sommerfeldt, Atle. "Forward." In *Waters of Life and Death: Ethical and Theological Responses to Contemporary Water Crises.* Edited by Sam Peedikayil Mathew & Chandran Paul Martin. Delhi: ISPCK & Chennai: UELCI, 2005.

Tillich, Paul. *The Protestant Era.* Chicago, Illinois: The University of Chicago Press, 1948.

Vandana, *Waters of Fire.* Madras: The Christian Literature Society, 1981.

Victus, Solomon. "A Theological Reflection on Water." In *Waters of Life and Death: Ethical and Theological Responses to Contemporary Water Crises.* Edited by Sam Peedikayil Mathew & Chandran Paul Martin. Delhi: ISPCK & Chennai: UELCI, 2005.

Victus, Solomon. "Water – A Privatized Commodity: An Overview of Recent Policies." In *Waters of Life and Death: Ethical and Theological Responses to Contemporary Water Crises.* Edited by Sam Peedikayil Mathew & Chandran Paul Martin. Delhi: ISPCK & Chennai: UELCI, 2005.

Vohra, B. B. *Managing India's Water Resources.* New Delhi: Indian National Trust for Art & Cultural Heritage, 1990.

Volf, Miroslav. "A Queen and a Beggar: Challenges and Prospects of Theology" (Introduction). In *The Future of Theology: Essays in Honor of Jurgen Moltmann.* Edited by Miroslav Volf, Carmen Krieg and Thomas Kucharz. Grand Rapids, Michigan: William B. Eerdmans Publishing Company, 1996.

Wielenga, Bas. *Towards an Eco-Just Society.* Bangalore: Centre for Social Action, 1999.

Wilkinson, Loren. *Earth Keeping in the Nineties: Stewardship of Creation.* Grand Rapids, Michigan: William B. Eerdmans Publishing Company, 1991.

Wilson, John. *The Parsi Religion.* Gurgaon, Haryana: Vintage Books, 1989.

Periodicals

Allison, Dale C. Jr. "The Living Water (John 4:10-14, 6:35c, 7:37-39)." *St Vladimir's Theological Quarterly* 30/2 (1986): 143-157.

Ariarajah, Wesley. "The Water of Life." *The Ecumenical Review* 34/3 (July 1982): 271-279.

Birch, Bruce C. "Old Testament Foundations for Peacemaking in the Nuclear Era." *The Christian Century* (December 4, 1985): 1115-1119.

Bloomer, Nancy. "The Ever-Moving Life Force," *The Living Pulpit* (January-March 2005): 22-23.

Campbell, Maura. "Symbol and Reality: Water, Life, Death and Christian Baptism." *Dialogue & Alliance* 4/1 (Spring 1990): 48-60.

Cho, Rebecca U. "Is bottled water a moral issue?" *Christian Century* (January 9, 2007): 13-14.

Day, John N. "God and Leviathan in Isaiah 27:1." *Bibliotheca Sacra* 155 (October-December 1998): 423-436.

Dhanaraj, D. "Integrity of Creation – A Theological Perspective." *The Sathri Journal* 1/1 (January 2006): 87-107.

Duchrow, Ulrich. "Private Property: A Growing Danger for life (or: Neglected in the Globalization Debate)." *Ecumenical Review* 54/4 (October 2002): 472-482. Fernandes, Walter. "Land, Water, Air as Community Livelihood: Impact of Globalization." *National Council of Churches Review* CXXII/1 (January-February 2002): 9-38.

________________. "The Draft Forest Policy 1987; the National Water Policy 1987." *Social Action* 38/1 (Jan-March): 84-94.

Flesher, LeAnn Snow. "Signs and Symbols – Water and Faith." *The Living Pulpit* (January-March 2005): 35-39.

Grab, Ginger (Compiler). "Quotations about Water." *The Living Pulpit* (January-March 2005): 48-49.

Grey, Mary. "Thirsty for Water - Thirsty for Life: Gender and Poverty in Rural Rajasthan." *Ecotheology* 9/1 (2004): 86-104.

Grula, John W. "Pantheism Reconstructed: Ecotheology as a Successor to the Judeo-Christian, Enlightenment, and Postmodernist Paradigms." *Zygon* 43/1 (March 2008): 159-180.

Hamilton, Mark W. "In the shadow of Leviathan: kingship in the book of Job." *Restoration Quarterly* 45/1-2 (2003): 29-40.

Jathanna, O. V. "Channels of Life: Engaging with Life-affirming, Life-negating and Life-renewing Realities." *Masihi Sevak* XXXII/2 (August 2007): 5-13.

Jayachitra, L. "A Postcolonial Exploration of Water in the Fourth Gospel." *Bangalore Theological Forum,* 37/2 (December 2005): 114-129.

Jeremiah, Anderson H. M. "Privatization of Water - A Theological Critique and Ensuing Challenges for the Church." *Reformed World* 57/1 (March 2007): 3-16.

Kennedy, S. M. John. "Pure Water is the Fundamental Right of All." *Journal of Dharma* 31/4 (October-December 2006): 485-496.

Kumar, Asha Krishna. "Women and Water," *Frontline* 20/20 (October 10, 2003): 78-80.

Kumar, G. Sathis and S. Ramaswamy. "Water for Sustainable Livelihood: Principles and Challenges." *Vikas Vani Journal* II/2 (April-June 2008): 61-69.

Mcguire, Errol M. "Yahweh and Leviathan: an exegesis of Isaiah 27:1." *Restoration Quarterly* 13/3 (1970): 165-179.

Miguez-Bonino, Jose. "For Life and Against Death: A Theology that Takes Sides." *Christian Century* (November 26, 1980): 1154-1158.

Morris, Henry M. "Water and the Word." *Bibliotheca Sacra* (July, 1961): 203-215.

Panwar, Vandana. "Techniques of Water Management and Conservation." *Vikas Vani Journal* II/2 (April-June 2008): 12-18.

Pushparajan, A. "Environmental Rights: Caring for God's Earth." *Indian Theological Studies* 43/1 (March 2006): 63-99.

Ramachandraiah, C. "Drinking Water as a Fundamental Right." *Economic and Political Weekly* (February 24, 2001): 619-621.

Rawlins, Clifford Reinhold Leandro. "Water, Source of Life – Socioeconomic, Theological and Interreligious Perspectives." *Reformed World* 57/1 (March 2007): 17-30.

Riege, Joerg. "The Economy is Expanding: Theology to the Rescue?" *Religious Studies Review* 28/3 (July 2002): 215-220.

Robra, Martin. "People's Struggle for Life are a source of inspiration for an enriching Spirituality." *National Council of Churches Review* CXXII/1 (January-February 2002): 3-8.

Saini, Angela. "Scarce 'blue gold'." *Frontline* (February 13, 2004): 37-38.

Seong-Won, Park. "Economy of Water: A Spiritual Basis for an Alternative Economy." *Ecumenical Review* 57/2 (April 2005): 171-178.

Tracy, David. "The Role of Theology in Public Life: Some Reflections." *Word and World* 4/3 (Summer 1984): 230-239.

Vaughn, John H. "If the Earth is the Lord's, Who Owns the Water?" *The Living Pulpit* (January-March 2005): 20-21._

Witcamp, L. TH. "Jesus' Thirst in John 19: 28-30: Literal or Figurative?" *Journal of Biblical Literature* 115/3 (1996): 489-510.

"Water for life," *Challenge Newsline*, Issue 60 (April 2006): 4.

"Water Sustains Life," *Statement on Water* (A Statement of the Conference on "Land, Water, Air – People Struggling for Life in a Globalizing Economy" held in Bangalore on 10-15 Dec. 2001), *National Council of Churches Review,* CXXII/1 (January – February 2002): 121-127.

Dictionaries, Encyclopedia and Commentaries

Alexander and Brian S. Rosner. Leicester, England: Inter-Varsity Press, 2000.

Boff, Leonardo. "Ecology." *Dictionary of Third World Theologies.* Edited by Virginia Fabella and R. S. Sugirtharajah. Maryknoll, New York: Orbis Books, 2000, 80-82.

Driver, Samuel Rolles and George Buchanan Gray. *A Critical and Exegetical Commentary on the Book of Job: International Critical Commentary*. Edinburgh Clark, 1977.

Eliade, Mircea and Lawrence E. Sullivan. "HIEROPHANY." *Encyclopedia of Religion*. Edited by Mircea Eliade. Vol. 6 (New York: Macmillan Publishing Company, 1987): 313-317.

Grassi, Joseph A. "Water." *The Collegevilla Pastoral Dictionary of Biblical Theology*. Bangalore: Theological Publications in India, 2005, 1060.

Marshall, I. H. "Myth." *New Dictionary of Theology*. Edited by Sinclain B. Ferguson and David F. Wright. Illinois: Inter-varsity Press, 1988, 449-451.

Rudhardt, Jean. "Water." *Encyclopedia of Religion*. Edited by Mircea Eliade. Vol.15 (New York: Macmillan Publishing Company, 1987): 350-358.

Smith, D. Moody. "John." *Harper's Bible Commentary*. Edited by James L. Mays. Harper San Francisco, New York, 1988, 1044-1076.

Tsumara, D. T. "Water." *New Dictionary of Biblical Theology*. Edited by Desmond.

Webliography

Abrams, Paula. *Water in Religions*, http://www.africanwater.org/religion.htm accessed on 25/07/2008.

Devraj, Ranjit. "Bypassing community rights: The National Water Policy," http://infochangeindia.org/ 200201015973/Water-Resources/Books-Reports/Bypassing-community-rights-The-National-Water-Policy.html accessed on 25/07/ 2008.

Weida, William J. "A General Economic Critique of Water Privatization," http://www.totse.com/en/politics/green_planet/164793.html accessed on 12/09/2008.

http://www.worldvision.com.au/stir/Content.aspx?topicID=478 accessed on 26/08/08.

http://www.worldvision.com.au/stir/Content.aspx?topicID=478 accessed on 26/08/08.

http://www.worldwaterinstitute.org/docs/executive%20summary%2022%20march%2 0meeting.pdf accessed on 25/07/ 2008.

http://www.citizen.org/cmep/Water/general accessed on 12/09/2008.

http://www.citizen.org/cmep/Water/articles.cfm?ID=10842accessed on 12/09/2008.

http://www.citizen.org/cmep/Water/articles.cfm?ID=10842accessed on 12/09/2008.

Unpublished Works

Franks, Martha. "The Need for a Theology of Water: the Drought of Spiritual Power in Environmental Law and Politics." An unpublished paper.

Joseph, Laisamma. "Doordarshan and Its Ecological Awareness Education." M.Sc. Thesis, Madurai Kamaraj University, 1998.

Joy, Joji K. "Symbolism of Water in the West Syrian Liturgy: An Interpretation from Biblical and Patristic Perspectives and Its Implication in the Modern Context." M.Th. Thesis, Senate of Serampore College, 1999.

Thambusamy, Samuel. "Rapid Urbanization in India and Its Impact on Drinking Water Resources: Towards an Action Plan for Engaging Children and Young People in Water Conservation in Chennai." An unpublished article.

Index

A

Alternate economy 86-87, 98
Anthropocentrism 60, 77, 93, 97

B

Baptism 16-18, 59-61, 73, 83, 95
Baptismal water 59
Biblical-theology 97
Bottled water 45, 54-56, 96
Buddhism 9, 95

C

Ceremonies 2-4, 10, 13-14
Children 2, 31, 35-36, 53, 71, 87, 96-97
Christianity 16-18, 95
Church 16-17, 77, 91-93, 98
Climate change 33-34, 54
Common heritage 50, 66-67
Community ownership 37, 88
Contamination 15, 21, 27, 30, 76
Creation 2, 5, 9-12, 18-19, 59-60, 62-63, 67-68, 70, 72-78, 80, 83, 87-88, 90, 94-98

D

Dalits 37, 53, 96
Development 22, 26, 40-44, 46, 48, 57, 88-89, 98
Dominion 60, 66
Dragon 67, 69-71
Drought 33-34, 43-44, 54, 63, 96

E

Eco-feminism 62-63
Ecological destruction 52
Ecology 48, 61-62
Eco-theology 61, 97
Environment 10, 29-30, 35, 40, 56, 79, 88
Eucharist 61
Eutrophication 30

F

Fertility 63, 82, 95
Flood 15-16, 24, 34, 42, 44, 96
Food security 21, 47-48, 79

G

Globalization 45, 65, 71, 75, 86, 92, 96, 98

H

Hinduism 2-3, 6, 95
Human Rights 37-38, 57, 74-76

I

Industrial wastes 28, 30
Interlinking of rivers 42-43
Islam 6, 8-9, 95

J

Judaism 15, 95

L

Leviathan 68-69, 71, 97
Life 2, 4-6, 9-11, 15, 17, 19, 21, 23, 25, 28-29, 31, 34, 36-41, 46-48, 53, 58-61, 63-65, 68, 70-75, 77-94, 96-98
Life-centeredness 77, 93, 97
Life-giving 4, 6, 19, 72, 74-75, 87, 95
Living water 15, 17, 63, 73-74, 83

N

National Water Policy 24, 36, 40-41
Natural rights 34, 38, 96
Neoliberal creeds 71
Neo-liberalism 86, 89
New life 61, 63

O

Ownership 37, 48-49, 66-68, 71, 88, 97

P

Pesticides 27, 29, 33, 96
Pollution 2, 10, 12, 18, 21-23, 25-30, 32, 34, 76, 92-93
Poor 23, 33, 38, 52-53, 55-56, 71, 76, 84-85, 93, 97
Precious commodity 58
Privatization of water 45-46, 48-53, 55, 57-58, 68, 71-72, 77-78, 86, 91, 93, 96-98
Process theology 60
Procreation 63
Purification 3, 6-8, 11, 13, 15, 17-18, 53, 95

R

Responsibility 36, 46, 62, 76-78, 80, 92, 98
Right to water 36-39

S

Sacred 1-3, 5, 9-11, 13-15, 18, 81, 95
Sacred bath 13-14
Salat 6-7
Sanitation 21, 26, 31, 33, 35-36, 45, 57-58, 82, 90, 92
Shalom 80, 89-90, 98
Sikhism 10, 95

Sin 6, 16-17, 73, 78, 83
Source of life 2, 19, 37, 63, 74, 80, 83, 90, 96
Springs of water 85
Stewardship 12, 62, 91, 97

T

Thirst 17, 48, 74-75, 77, 83, 93
Thirsts for life 75
Transnational Corporations 51, 54
Tribals 37, 44, 53, 96

V

Varuna 12, 18, 95

W

Water
- Agent for justice 56
- As a commodity, 50, 55
- Consecrated water, 11, 13
- Drinking water, 21, 25, 28-29, 31-33, 39-41, 43-49, 53-55, 64, 67, 84, 89, 91-94, 96
- Free resource 91
- Fresh water, 21, 28, 30, 33, 53-54, 63, 72, 76-77, 79, 82-83
- Ground water, 22-25, 33, 46, 51, 53-54, 85, 96
- Holy water, 17
- Living water, 15, 17, 63, 73-74, 83
- Progenitor, 10
- Pure water, 8
- Rainwater, 24-25, 91
- Sanctified water, 9
- Symbol 5-6, 9, 18, 63, 68, 71, 73-74, 80-81, 83-84, 95

Water conflicts 34-35, 44
Water crisis 21-23, 91, 94
Water is life 74-75
Water management 23-25, 35-36, 41, 50, 88
Water of life 47-48, 63, 72, 74, 83, 97
Water pricing 40
Water resources 23-24, 30, 32-33, 37, 39, 40-41, 44, 48-50, 55-56, 67, 71, 80, 84-86, 88-89, 94, 96
Water scarcity 21, 32, 44, 46, 48, 94
Water-borne diseases 31
Women 14-15, 35-37, 53, 63, 71, 85, 96-97

Z

Zoroastrianism 10, 12-15, 95